Illustrations by Hannah D. Block

Cooking with CHEESE

Culinary Arts Institute®

A DIVISION OF DELAIR PUBLISHING COMPANY, INC.

ISBN: 0-8326-0632-4

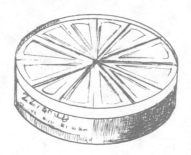

Contents

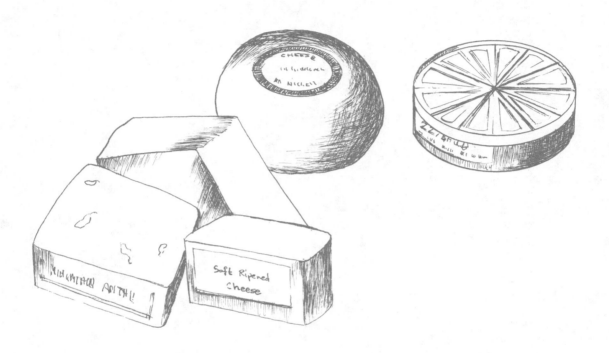

Cheese & Cheese Cookery

The TRUE CHEESE-LOVER can get pleasure from simply reading about cheese, as a musician derives excitement from reading a score. For most of us, however, the joy of cheese is in the tasting. An English gourmet once said that "the only way to learn about cheese is to eat it," and for some 4,000 years of recorded history people have been doing just that.

No one knows just how or when cheese was discovered. The ancient Greeks esteemed it so highly that they believed it to be a gift of the gods. Legend has it that it was discovered quite by accident when an Arab traveler carried as part of his food supply on a journey across the desert some milk in a crude container fashioned from a sheep's stomach. By some happy chance the heat of the day and the rennet still remaining in the container caused the milk to separate into curds and whey. The whey satisfied the traveler's thirst and the curd his appetite—and so cheese was born.

Few foods equal cheese for nutritive value and variety of flavor and texture. More than 350 different cheeses have been catalogued and described, oftentimes in accents of rapture. Cheese is produced and prized around the world. It serves more purposes than can be listed here. It can be used as appetizer, entree or dessert, and the magic of its flavor—its many flavors—combines enchantingly with many other foods. Cooking with cheese is a fascinating and rewarding adventure. Success is certain if two simple rules are kept in mind: As a protein food, cheese requires a low temperature; and it must not be overcooked.

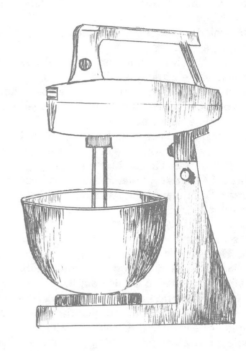

It's Smart to Be Careful

There's No Substitute for Accuracy

Read recipe carefully.

Assemble all ingredients and utensils.

Select pans of proper kind and size. Measure inside, from rim to rim.

Use standard measuring cups and spoons. Use measuring cups with subdivisions marked on sides for liquids. Use graduated nested measuring cups for dry or solid ingredients.

Check liquid measurements at eye level.

Level dry or solid measurements with straight-edged knife or spatula.

Sift (before measuring) regular all-purpose flour, or not, in accord with the miller's directions on the package. When using the instant type all-purpose flour, follow package directions and recipes. Level flour in cup with straight-edged knife or spatula. Spoon, without sifting, whole-grain types of flour into measuring cup.

Preheat oven at required temperature.

Beat whole eggs until thick and softly piled when recipe calls for well-beaten eggs.

For These Recipes—What To Use

Baking Powder—double-action type.

Bread cubes—two slices fresh bread equal about 1 cup soft crumbs or cubes. One slice dry or toasted bread equals about ½ cup dry cubes or ¼ cup fine, dry crumbs.

Buttered Crumbs—soft or dry bread or cracker crumbs tossed in melted butter or margarine. Use 1 to 2 tablespoons butter or margarine for 1 cup soft crumbs or 2 to 4 tablespoons butter or margarine for 1 cup dry crumbs.

Chocolate—unsweetened chocolate. A general substitution for 1 sq. (1 oz.) chocolate is 3 to 4 tablespoons cocoa plus 1 tablespoon shortening.

Chocolate (no melt)—1-oz. packets or envelopes chocolate-flavored product or ingredient.

Cornstarch—thickening agent having double the thickening power of flour.

Cream—light, table or coffee cream, containing 18% to 20% butterfat.

Heavy or Whipping Cream—containing not less than 30% butterfat.

Flour—regular or all-purpose flour. When substituting for cake flour, use 1 cup minus 2 tablespoons all-purpose flour for 1 cup cake flour.

Grated Peel—whole citrus fruit peel finely grated through colored part only.

Herbs and Spices—ground unless recipe specifies otherwise.

Oil—salad or cooking type. Use olive oil only when recipe so directs.

Rotary Beater—hand operated (Dover type) beater, or use electric mixer.

Shortening—hydrogenated vegetable shortening, all-purpose shortening, butter or margarine. Use lard or oil when specified.

Sour Milk—cold sweet milk added to 1 tablespoon vinegar or lemon juice in a measuring cup to fill to 1-cup line; stir. Or use buttermilk.

Stuffed Olives—pimiento-stuffed olives.

Sugar granulated (either cane or beet).

Vinegar—cider vinegar, or as specified.

How to Do It

Bath, Hot Water—set a baking pan on oven rack and place the filled baking dish in pan. Surround with very hot water to a 1-in. depth.

Blanch Almonds and Pistachios—the flavor and crisp texture of nuts are best maintained when the nuts are allowed to remain in water the shortest possible time during blanching. Therefore, blanch only about 1/2 cup at a time; repeat as many times as necessary for larger amounts.

Bring to a rapid boil enough water to cover the shelled nuts. Drop nuts into water. Turn off heat and allow nuts to remain in water about 1 min., drain or lift out with slotted spoon or fork. Place between folds of absorbent paper; pat dry. Squeeze nuts between thumb and fingers to remove skins; or peel. Place on dry absorbent paper; to dry thoroughly, shift frequently to dry spots on paper.

Toast Nuts—place nuts in a shallow baking pan. Heat nuts (plain or brushed lightly with cooking oil) in oven at 350°F until delicately browned. Move and turn occasionally with fork. Or put nuts into a heavy skillet in which butter or margarine (about 1 tablespoon per cup of nuts) has been melted; or use oil. Heat until nuts are lightly browned, moving constantly with fork, over moderate heat. Drain on absorbent paper.

Salt Nuts—toast nuts; sprinkle with salt.

Boil—cook in liquid in which bubbles rise continually and break on the surface. Boiling temperature of water at sea level is 212°F.

Chill Gelatin—set dissolved gelatin mixture in refrigerator or in pan of ice and water until slightly thicker than consistency of thick, unbeaten egg white, or until mixture begins to gel (gets slightly thicker). If mixture is placed over ice and water, stir frequently; if placed in refrigerator, stir occasionally.

Clean Celery—trim off root end and cut off leaves. Leaves may be chopped and used for added flavor in soups and stuffings; inner leaves may be left on stalk when serving as relish. Separate stalks, remove blemishes and wash.

Clean Garlic—separate into cloves and remove thin, papery outer skin.

Clean Green Pepper—rinse and slice away from pod and stem; trim off any white membrane; rinse away seeds; cut into strips, dice or prepare as directed in recipe.

Clean and Slice Mushrooms—wipe with a clean, damp cloth and cut off tips of stems; slice lengthwise through stems and caps.

Clean Onions (dry)—cut off root end and a thin slice from stem end; peel and rinse. Prepare as directed in recipe.

Prepare Crumbs—put cookies, crackers, zwieback or dry bread on a long length of heavy waxed paper. Loosely fold paper around them, tucking open ends under. With rolling pin, gently crush to make fine crumbs. Or place cookies or crackers in a plastic bag and gently crush.

If using electric blender, break 5 or 6 pieces (cookies, crackers, etc.) into blender container. Cover container. Blend on low speed, flicking motor on and off, until crumbs are medium fine. Empty container and repeat.

Cut Dried Fruits (uncooked) or Marshmallows—cut with scissors dipped frequently in water.

Dice—cut into small cubes.

Flake Fish—with a fork, separate canned or cooked fish into flakes (thin, layer-like pieces). Remove bony tissue from crab meat; salmon bones are edible.

Flute Edge of Pastry—press index finger on edge of pastry, then pinch pastry with thumb and index finger of other hand. Lift fingers and repeat procedure to flute entire edge.

Fold—use flexible spatula. Slip it down side of bowl to bottom. Turn bowl quarter turn. Lift spatula through mixture along side of bowl with blade parallel to surface. Turn spatula over so as to fold lifted material across the surface. Cut down and under again; turn bowl and repeat process until material is blended. With every fourth stroke, bring spatula up through center.

Grate Nuts or Chocolate—use a rotary-type grater with hand-operated crank. Follow manufacturer's directions. Grated nuts or chocolate should be fine and light; do not use an electric blender for grating or grinding nuts called for in these recipes.

Hard-Cook Eggs—put eggs into large saucepan

and cover completely with cold or lukewarm water. Cover pan. Bring water rapidly just to boiling. Turn off heat immediately; if necessary to prevent further boiling, remove pan from heat source. Let eggs stand, covered, 20 to 22 min. Plunge eggs into cold, running water. Crackle shells and roll between hands to loosen shells. When cooled, start peeling at large end.

Marinate—allow food to stand in liquid (usually oil and acid) to impart flavor.

Measure Brown Sugar—pack firmly into dry measuring cup; sugar should hold shape of cup when turned out.

Measure Granulated Brown Sugar—*see* substitution table on package before pouring into measuring cup.

Mince—cut or chop into small, fine pieces.

Melt Chocolate, unsweetened, over simmering water; sweet or semi-sweet, over hot (not simmering) water.

Panbroil Bacon—place in a cold skillet only as many bacon slices as will lie flat. Cook slowly, turning frequently. Pour off fat as it collects. When bacon is evenly crisped and browned, remove from skillet and drain on absorbent paper.

Prepare Quick Broth—dissolve in 1 cup hot water, 1 chicken bouillon cube for chicken broth or 1 beef bouillon cube (or ½ teaspoon concentrated meat extract) for meat broth.

Rice—force through ricer, sieve or food mill.

Scald Milk—heat in top of double boiler over simmering water or in a heavy saucepan over direct heat just until a thin film appears.

Sieve—force through sieve or food mill.

Simmer—cook in a liquid just below boiling point; bubbles form slowly, break below surface.

Sweeten Whipped Cream—beat thoroughly chilled whipping cream in chilled bowl with chilled rotary beater; beat until cream stands in peaks when beater is slowly lifted upright. With final strokes, beat in 3 tablespoons sifted confectioners' sugar and 1 teaspoons vanilla extract for each cup of whipping cream.

Unmold Gelatin—run tip of knife around top edge of mold to loosen. Invert mold on chilled plate. If necessary, wet a clean towel in hot water and wring it almost dry. Wrap hot towel around mold for a few seconds only. (If mold does not loosen, repeat.)

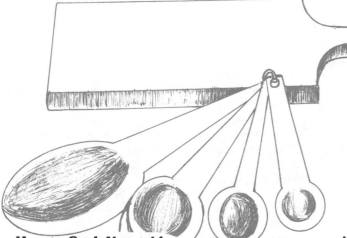

How to Cook Vegetables

Wash fresh vegetables, but do not allow them to stand in water for any length of time. An exception is cauliflower, which may be immersed in icy-cold salted water 3 or 4 minutes.

Have water boiling rapidly before adding vegetables. Add salt at beginning of cooking period (¼ teaspoon per cup of water). After adding vegetables, again bring water to boiling as quickly as possible. If more water is needed, add boiling water. Boil at moderate rate until vegetables are just tender; then drain and serve.

In general, cook vegetables in a covered pan, in the smallest possible amount of water and as quickly as possible. Exceptions for vegetables used in the following recipes are:

Asparagus—arranged in tied bundles with stalks standing in bottom of a double broiler containing water to cover lower half of spears; cover with inverted double-boiler top.

Cauliflower—Cook in a large amount of water in a loosely covered pan.

Oven Temperatures

Very Slow	250° to 275°F
Slow	300° to 325°F
Moderate	350° to 375°F
Hot	400° to 425°F
Very Hot	450° to 475°F
Extremely Hot	500° to 525°F

Use a portable oven thermometer to double check oven temperature.

When You Deep Fry

About 20 min. before deep frying, fill a deep saucepan one-half to two-thirds full with hydrogenated vegetable shortening, all-purpose shortening, lard or cooking oil. Heat fat slowly to temperature given in the recipe. A deep-frying thermometer is the most accurate guide to correct frying temperatures.

If thermometer is not available, this bread-cube test may be used as a guide: A 1-in. cube of white bread browns in 60 seconds when the temperature is 350° to 365°F.

When using an automatic deep fryer, follow manufacturer's directions for amount of fat.

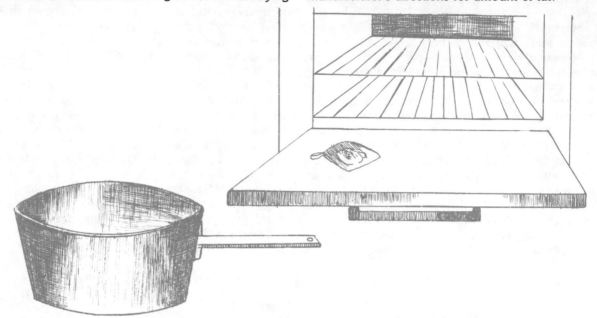

A Check-List for Successful Baking

✔**Read Again** "It's Smart To Be Careful—There's No Substitute for Accuracy," page 9.

✔**Place Oven Rack** so center-top of product will be almost at center of oven.

✔**Have All Ingredients** at room temperature unless recipe directs otherwise.

✔**Sift** (before measuring) regular all-purpose flour, or not, in accord with the miller's directions on the package. When using the instant type all-purpose flour, follow package directions and recipes. Level flour in cup with straight-edged knife or spatula. Spoon, without sifting, whole-grain types of flour into measuring cup.

✔**Cream Shortening** (alone or with flavorings) by stirring rubbing or beating with spoon or electric mixer until softened. Add sugar in small amounts, creaming thoroughly after each addition. Thorough creaming helps to insure a fine-grained cake.

✔**Beat Egg Yolks** until thick and lemon-colored when recipe calls for well-beaten egg yolks.

✔**Beat Egg Whites** as follows: **Frothy**—entire mass forms bubbles; **Rounded peaks**—peaks turn over slightly when beater is slowly lifted upright; **Stiff peaks**—peaks remain standing when beater is slowly lifted upright.

✔**Beat Whole Eggs** until thick and softly piled when recipe calls for well-beaten eggs.

✔**When Liquid and Dry Ingredients** are added alternately to batters and mixtures, begin and end with dry. Add dry ingredients in fourths, liquid in thirds. After each addition, beat only until smooth. Finally, beat only until batter is smooth (do not overbeat). Scrape spoon or beater and bottom and sides of bowl during mixing.

If using an electric mixer, beat mixture at low speed when alternately adding liquid and dry ingredients.

✔**Test** for lukewarm liquid (80°F to 85°F) by placing a drop on wrist; it should feel neither hot nor cold.

✔**Knead Dough** by folding opposite edge over toward you. Using heels of hands, gently push dough away. Give it a quarter turn. Repeat process rhythmically until the dough becomes smooth and elastic, 5 to 8 min., using a little additional flour as possible. Always turn the dough in the same direction.

✔**Remove Rolls, Breads and Cookies** from pans as they come from the oven, unless otherwise directed. Set on cooling racks to cool.

✔**Keep Tops** of yeast loaves and rolls soft by immediately brushing them with butter as they come from the oven.

A Check-List for Cheese

✔**Cook Cheese** over low heat to prevent toughening, stringing and separation. Use double boiler or chafing pan when recipe so directs. On some ranges with very low heating potentials, cheese can be cooked over low direct heat.

✔**Grate Cheese** with a rotary-type grater with hand-operated crank. Follow manufacturer's directions. One-half pound cheese will yield about 2 cups grated or shredded.

✔**Shred Cheese** with a standard kitchen shredder. Size of perforation to use will depend on kind of cheese and intended use. For garnish, cheese shreds should be long and fluffy.

✔**Slice Cheese** with a wire cheese slicer for best results. Or use a sharp, thin-bladed knife.

✔**Soften Cream Cheese** at room temperature until soft enough to handle as required.

✔**Thin Cream Cheese** with milk or cream until desired consistency is obtained. Or use fruit juice for added flavor.

✔**Store Hard Cheeses** (such as Cheddar and Swiss) in the refrigerator, wrapping tightly in aluminum foil or moisture-vapor-proof material to prevent drying. **Mold development** during storage is a normal process. Scrape or cut mold from surface, discard it and use remainder of cheese.

✔**Store Soft, Uncured Cheeses** (cottage cheese and cream cheese) in the refrigerator for a short period of time. Cream cheese should be tightly wrapped in its original wrapper, or in aluminum foil or moisture-vapor proof material; cottage cheese should be stored in a tightly covered container.

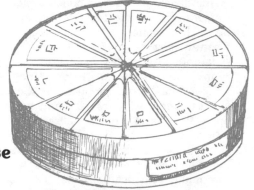

A Guide to Cheese

MAN HAS BEEN MAKING CHEESE since recorded history began, and probably longer. In different parts of the world, different kinds of milk and different methods of handling the cheese have produced many different and distinctive types. As people of many races came to the United States, they brought the knowledge of and the taste for native cheeses with them. As a result, many kinds of cheese which originated in many lands are today being produced in this country, and a good many of them are also imported from their native lands and made available to American homemakers.

A few, such as Roquefort or Blue, Swiss, Parmesan and, most of all, Cheddar, have become so thoroughly domesticated here that almost everyone knows them and has used them at some time. But others, which offer a great deal of new eating pleasure, are not yet very widely known. In The Cheese Dictionary you will find brief introductions to the most widely distributed cheeses, each with its own special characteristics and uses.

These cheese varieties are *natural cheeses*, made directly from milk, with or without aging and "ripening" by bacterial action or molds. Natural cheese is purchased in cuts made from the big "wheels" and other forms; it is also available pre-cut into slices,

wedges and convenient-shaped pieces and pre-wrapped in air-tight packages. Natural cheeses made domestically are often made in loaves or bricks which would not be recognized in the native lands of the cheeses.

In recent years cheese has also been available in various other newly developed forms:

Process cheese—produced from natural cheeses blended for uniformity of flavor, texture and cooking quality. The cheeses are ground together, melted, pasteurized and poured into molds lined with moisture-vapor-proof packaging material; the packages are sealed and the cheese, virtually sterilized, is cooled in the packages. Process cheese has typically a perfectly smooth consistency and good keeping quality.

Cheese food—may be either *process,* made like process cheese but with certain dairy products added; or *cold-pack,* with the same additions but not pasteurized. The process type is perfectly smooth; the cold-pack type is somewhat granular and crumbly because it is not homogenized.

Process cheese spreads—cheese foods of a slightly higher moisture content to produce a more spreadable consistency at room temperature.

The Cheese Dictionary

Bel Paese
A soft, creamy cheese with a firm rind and moderately sharp flavor. With crackers, it is a pleasing addition to the cheese tray.

Blue
Similar to Roquefort; made from cows' milk as a domestic variety.

Brick
A real American cheese, semisoft and ranging from very mild to moderately sharp in flavor. A much favored sandwich and buffet cheese.

Brie
An older French variety of Bel Paese.

Caciocavallo
A spindle-shaped Italian cheese, piquant in flavor, similar to Provolone. May be used in the same manner as Provolone.

Camembert
A famous French dessert cheese. Very soft, almost runny, with pungent flavor. Bring it to room temperature before serving; eat the rind with the cheese. Serve with crackers and fruit; delicious on apple slices or in a hot appetizer.

Cheddar
A firm, flavorful cheese supposed to have originated in the village of Cheddar, England; it has become so thoroughly Americanized that it is often known as "American" cheese. About 75 percent of all the cheese made in this country is Cheddar, varying in flavor from very mild to very sharp, depending on length of aging and ripening period. Used for sandwiches, in cooked dishes, on cheese trays and often for dessert.

Cottage Cheese
A soft, uncured cheese, usually made from skim milk. It is always eaten fresh (it can be kept two to three days in the refrigerator, but not longer. Cover tightly.) A versatile cheese, it is used in salads, with fruits, and in certain cooked or baked dishes, such as the cheese cakes.

Cream Cheese
A soft, uncured cheese, made from cream or a mixture of milk and cream. It is very mild in flavor, must be eaten fresh, may be eaten alone as a rich, delicate spread on crisp, salty crackers or blended with more flavorful foods, and is often used, softened and sweetened, as cake topping. A most versatile cheese, it is also useful in cooking.

Edam
A semisoft to hard cheese usually made in a cannonball shape; it is a native Dutch cheese, with a mild, slightly salty flavor. A bright red rind is characteristic of Edam. The rind of imported Edam is colored and the cheese is then wrapped in transparent film; domestic Edams are usually covered in red paraffin or a tightly adhering red plastic film. A delightful table cheese, it is usually served on a cheese tray with the top cut off so the interior may be scooped out and spread on crisp crackers.

Gjetost
A Norwegian cheese made from goats' milk whey, or more commonly from whey obtained when cheese is made from a mixture of goats' and cows' milk. A rather mild cheese with a sweetish flavor, a firm buttery consistency and a golden brown in color. Most typically used for smorgasbord service, almost always with dark bread, as a pleasing contrast to more familiar cheese.

Gorgonzola
The Italian equivalent of Roquefort and Blue.

Gouda
Very similar to Edam, usually shaped like a flattened ball. Though Goudas may weigh as much as 50 pounds, "Baby" Goudas weighing about one pound are more familiar in this country. The rind is usually (but not invariably) red. A popular dessert cheese.

Gruyère
A Swiss cheese with smaller holes and sharper flavor. Delicious for sandwiches, dessert, on the cheese tray, or in fondue.

Herkimer
A sharp, aged Cheddar cheese produced in New York State; it originated in Herkimer county. It is a pale creamy-yellow in color, rather dry and crumbly, sharp in flavor, with excellent cooking quality. Fine for sandwiches, dessert, the cheese tray and for all cooking.

Liederkranz
A soft, surface-ripened cheese, it is creamy-white and mildly pungent. It is a native American variety, produced by one company only. Fine with crackers or rye bread, on the cheese tray, and served with beer.

Limburger
Resembles Liederkranz in texture, but with a much stronger flavor and aroma.

Liptauer
A Hungarian cheese, made from the milk of the sheep that browse in the Carpathian mountains. In Hungary the cheese is mixed with sharp seasonings and eaten on dark bread as an appetizer.

Mozzarella
A fresh, unsalted, white, moist cheese with a delicate flavor; it may be eaten sliced or used in baked dishes. Imported Mozzarella cheeses are sometimes spherical in shape.

Mysost

Similar to Gjetost, but made from cows' milk. Some Mysost is made domestically, whereas most Gjetost is still imported.

Neufchâtel

Similar in flavor and texture to cream cheese, but with a lower fat content. Used in the same ways. A popular dessert cheese.

Parmesan

A very hard cheese when fully cured, used only for grating in this country; in Italy it is also used when partially cured as a table cheese. Parmesan is the grated cheese without which Italian dishes are incomplete; it is sprinkled over these at the table, but its piquant flavor makes it a desirable ingredient in many cooked dishes and sauces the world over.

Provolone

A firm, smooth, pear-shaped cheese, usually smoked. A table cheese when partially cured; suitable for grating when fully cured and dried.

Ricotta

A mild Italian cheese usually used in cooking. It is marketed either fresh and moist (like a smooth cottage cheese) or dry; suitable for grating.

Romano

Similar to Parmesan and used much in the same manner.

Roquefort

The original French version of blue-veined cheese. Only cheese made from ewes' milk in the Roquefort area of France, and cured in the caves of that district, may be called Roquefort; therefore all Roquefort is imported. The chracteristic flavor is sharp and slightly peppery. The cured cheese is firm but crumbly, with blue-green veins of mold (Penicillium roqueforti) throughout. Delicious for salads, appetizer spread and for dessert.

Sapsago

A hard cheese made in Switzerland, colored green by the addition of powdered dried clover leaves. Suitable for grating; when grated it is used in cooking. Mixed with butter, it is a delicious spread.

Scamorze

Similar to Mozzarella. Either of these two Italian cheeses may be used for pizza.

Swiss

A hard, almost white cheese with elastic body, immediately recognizable by large eyes (gas holes), up to 1 inch in diameter, which develop in the curd as the cheese ripens. The flavor is mild and nut-like; imported Swiss has more pronounced flavor due to longer ripening. A favorite for sandwiches; it toasts well, is delicious in cooked dishes and adds eye-appeal and flavor to the cheese tray. Slice rather thick to compensate for holes.

Trappist

A soft, creamy cheese, known also as Oka and Port-Salut and made in Trappist monasteries around the world from a secret formula of the order.

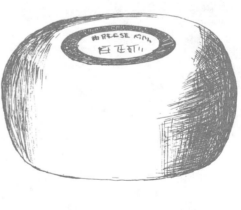

Appetizers

Special Blender Cheese Dip

¼   **lb. Blue cheese, crumbled**
3   **oz. (1 pkg.) cream cheese**
¼   **cup thick sour cream**
2   **tablespoons pineapple juice**
2   **teaspoons Worcestershire sauce**
1   **drop Tabasco**
5   **sprigs parsley**
1   **slice onion**

1. Put Blue cheese, cream cheese, sour cream, pineapple juice, Worcestershire sauce, Tabasco, parsley, and onion into blender container.
2. Cover and turn on motor. Blend until smooth.

About 1½ cups dip

Clam Appetizer Dip

1   **10-oz. can clams**
6   **oz. cream cheese**
1   **tablespoon lemon juice**
1   **teaspoon Worcestershire sauce**
½   **teaspoon salt**
⅛   **teaspoon finely ground pepper**
1   **sliver garlic**

1. Drain clams, reserving ¼ cup liquid.
2. Put reserved liquid into blender container with cream cheese, lemon juice, Worcestershire sauce, salt, ground pepper, and garlic.
3. Cover and turn on motor. Add clams; blend.

About 2 cups dip

Devilish Cheese Dip: Follow recipe for Clam Appetizer Dip. Omit clams and clam liquid. Increase cream cheese to 8 oz. Add 2¼-oz. can **deviled ham** and ½ cup **mayonnaise.**

Bean-Olive Dunk

6   oz. cream cheese, softened
2   teaspoons lemon juice
1   teaspoon grated lemon peel
1   10½- to 11-oz. can condensed black bean soup
⅔   cup chopped black olives

1. Beat cream cheese, lemon juice and lemon peel together until fluffy.
2. Mix in contents of black bean soup.
3. Stir in olives.
4. Chill thoroughly.

About 2 cups dunk

Avocado-Cottage Cheese Dip

1   cup cream-style cottage cheese
1   large ripe avocado
2   teaspoons lemon juice
3   tablespoons minced parsley
2   teaspoons grated onion
½   teaspoon salt
¼   teaspoon pepper
1   clove garlic, minced; or crushed in a garlic press
    Paprika

1. Force cottage cheese through a sieve or food mill and set aside.
2. Rinse, cut into halves and remove pit from avocado.
3. Carefully scoop fruit from shells, reserving the shells to use as containers for serving the dip. Put the avocado into a bowl and mash well with a fork. Blend in lemon juice.
4. Mix in the sieved cottage cheese and parsley, onion, salt, pepper, and garlic.
5. Blend until ingredients are thoroughly mixed. Spoon the dip into the reserved shells. Set in refrigerator to chill.
6. Before serving, sprinkle with paprika.
7. Accompany with slices and pieces of assorted fresh vegetables, potato chips or crackers. Arrange all attractively on an hors d'oeuvre tray and garnish with a few sprigs of parsley.

About 2 cups dip

Note: For a smooth dip, beat the avocado with an electric mixer. Gradually add cottage cheese and seasonings and blend smooth.

Cream-Cheese "Liptauer" Spread

2   anchovy fillets
1   slice onion
8   oz. cream cheese, softened
3   tablespoons thick sour cream
½   cup butter or margarine, softened
1   tablespoon prepared mustard
1½ teaspoons paprika
1   teaspoon caraway seeds
1   teaspoon capers
½   teaspoon salt

1. Finely chop anchovy fillets and onion.
2. Beat together cream cheese, sour cream, and butter or margarine until well blended.
3. Add with anchovy and onion and mix well mustard, paprika, caraway seeds, capers, and salt.
4. Beat until smooth.
5. Transfer "Lipatauer" spread to a serving dish and shape into a smooth mound. Sprinkle with paprika and chill in refrigerator.
6. To garnish, arrange parsley sprigs around cheese mound and insert a few rolled anchovy fillets on wooden picks into mound.

1¾ cups spread

Cottage Cheese: Follow recipe for Cream-Cheese "Liptauer" Spread. Substitute 1 cup **cream-style cottage chese** for cream cheese.

Fabulous Cheese Mousse

¼	cup cold water
1	env. unflavored gelatin
3	1¼-oz. pkgs. Roquefort cheese
2	1⅓-oz. pkgs. Camembert cheese
1	egg yolk, slightly beaten
1	tablespoon sherry
1	teaspoon Worcestershire sauce
1	egg white
½	cup chilled whipping cream
	Stuffed olive slices

1. Set out a fancy 1-pt. mold. Put a small bowl and a hand rotary beater into refrigerator to chill.
2. Pour water into a small cup or custard cup.
3. Sprinkle unflavored gelatin evenly over cold water.
4. Let stand until softened.
5. Dissolve gelatin completely by placing over very hot water.
6. Force Roquefort cheese and Camembert cheese through a fine sieve.
7. Blend egg yolk, sherry, and Worcestershire sauce in until mixture is smooth.
8. Add dissolved gelatin to cheese mixture, blending thoroughly.
9. Beat egg white until rounded peaks are formed.
10. Using the chilled bowl and beater, beat whipping cream until cream is of medium consistency (piles softly).
11. Fold the whipped cream and egg white into the cheese mixture. Turn into the mold. Chill in refrigerator until firm.
12. Unmold onto chilled serving plate. Garnish with olive slices.
13. Serve with **crackers.**

One 1-pt. mold

Saucy Biscuit Surprises

	Cheese Fans (page 28; omit cheese)
1	roll (6 oz.) sharp Cheddar cheese food with garlic
	Milk

1. Prepare dough for Cheese Fans.
2. Roll ¼ in. thick and cut into 1½- in. rounds. Place half of the rounds about 1 in. apart on a baking sheet.
3. Thinly slice Cheddar cheese.
4. Place one slice on each round; cover with another round. Brush tops with milk.
5. Bake at 450°F 10 to 15 min., or until biscuits are golden brown.

15 to 18 1½-in. biscuits

Southern Cheese Log

1	cup (about 4 oz.) pecans
2	cloves garlic
6	oz. cream cheese, softened
⅛	teaspoon Worcestershire sauce
⅛	teaspoon Maggi's seasoning
⅛	teaspoon salt
4	drops Tabasco
1½	teaspoons chili powder

1. Put pecans and garlic through medium blade of food chopper.
2. Put cream cheese, Worcestershire sauce, seasoning, salt, and Tabasco into a bowl and blend together thoroughly.
3. Blend in the pecan-garlic mixture. Shape the cheese mixture into a roll about 5 in. long and about 1½ in. in diameter.
4. Sprinkle chili powder evenly over a sheet of waxed paper.
5. Roll the log in the chili powder, coating it evenly. Wrap tightly in waxed paper or moisture-vapor-proof material. Chill in refrigerator until cheese log is firm and flavors are blended (about 4 hrs.).
6. Serve with crisp **crackers.**

One cheese log.

Nippy Cheddar Savories

4	oz. sharp Cheddar cheese (about 1 cup, shredded)
¼	cup butter
2	tablespoons mayonnaise
1	teaspoon prepared mustard
1	teaspoon lemon juice
¼	teaspoon celery salt
	Few grains white pepper
12	thin slices white or whole wheat bread

1. *For Cheese Butter* — Shred Cheddar cheese.
2. Cream butter until softened.
3. Gradually blend in the cheese. Beat until mixture is fluffy. Thoroughly blend in mayonnaise, prepared mustard, lemon juice, salt, and white pepper.
4. *For Savories* — Trim crusts from bread.
5. Flatten slightly with a rolling pin. (Bread slices are easier to roll up, if flattened slightly.) Generously spread each slice with about 1 tablespoon of the Cheese Butter. Roll up tightly and cut each roll into halves. Fasten with wooden picks; place on broiler rack.
6. Set temperature control of range at Broil. Place rack in broiler with tops of savories about 3 in. from soure of heat. Broil about 2 min., or until toasted.

24 Nippy Cheddar Savories

Cheese-Scallion Savories: Follow recipe for Nippy Cheddar Savories. Omit mayonnaise, mustard and lemon juice. Blend 1 tablespoon minced **scallion** and ½ teaspoon **Worcestershire sauce** into the fluffy cheese mixture.

Tangy Cheese Dip

3	cups (about ¾ lb.) grated sharp Cheddar cheese
⅓	cup (about 1¼ oz.) crumbled Roquefort or Blue cheese
¾	cup beer (measured without foam)
1	tablespoon butter or margarine, softened
1½	teaspoons grated onion
¾	teaspoon dry mustard
½	teaspoon Worcestershire sauce
2	drops Tabasco

1. Prepare Cheddar cheese and Roquefort or Blue cheese and mix together in a bowl.
2. Add beer gradually, stirring constantly until mixture is smooth.
3. Blend in butter or margarine, onion, dry mustard, Worcestershire sauce, and Tabasco.
4. Cover and chill thoroughly in refrigerator.

About 2 cups dip

Snappy Cocktail Spritz

½	lb. New York Herkimer cheese or any sharp Cheddar cheese
1	cup sifted all-purpose flour
¾	teaspoon paprika
¼	teaspoon cayenne pepper
¼	cup butter or margarine

1. Finely grate cheese into a bowl.
2. Cover and set aside overnight.
3. Set out a baking sheet.
4. Sift together flour, paprika, and cayenne pepper.
5. Set aside.
6. Cream butter or margarine until softened.
7. Thoroughly mix in the grated cheese. Mixing until well blended after each addition, add dry ingredients in fourths.
8. Using pastry bag and No. 7 star tube, squeeze 1½- to 2-in. lengths of mixture onto baking sheet. Or squeeze into any spritz cookie shape.
9. Bake at 375°F 10 to 15 min., or until delicately browned.

About 2 doz. cheese sticks

Appetizer Kabobs

1	9-oz. can pitted ripe olives
1	5-oz. jar sharp process cheese spread
2	teaspoons prepared horse-radish
1	teaspoon chili powder
1	teaspoon prepared mustard
¼	teaspoon salt
2	drops Tabasco
	Pickled onions
	Cocktail sausages
	Pineapple chunks
	Cooked shrimp

1. Skewers will be needed.
2. Set out can pitted ripe olives to drain.
3. Meanwhile, blend together contents of cheese spread and horse-radish, chili powder, prepared mustard, salt, and Tabasco.
4. Using the point of a small knife, fill each olive with cheese mixture.
5. *For Kabobs*—Set out in small bowls the stuffed olives and onions, sausages, pineapple chunks, and shrimp.
6. Thread any combination of the ingredients on skewers.
7. Set temperature control of range at Broil (500°F or higher); or heat hibachi according to manufacturer's directions.
8. Arrange Kabobs on broiler rack. Set rack in broiler with tops of Kabobs about 2 in. from source of heat. Turning frequently, broil Kabobs about 5 min., or until thoroughly heated. Serve hot.

Cheese "Croutons"

3	tablespoons butter or margarine
1½	cups bite-size shredded wheat biscuits
½	cup (2 oz.) grated Parmesan cheese

1. Melt butter or margarine over low heat in a medium-size skillet.
2. Add wheat biscuits.
3. Heat for 5 min., constantly turning biscuits gently with a spoon. Remove from heat. Add Parmesan cheese, tossing gently to coat biscuits.
4. Serve warm or cool. Store in tightly covered jar in refrigerator.

1½ cups "croutons"

Hot Camembert Morsels

3 1⅓-oz. pkgs. Camembert cheese
3 oz. (1 pkg.) cream cheese
¾ cup milk
¼ cup sifted all-purpose flour
2 tablespoons softened butter
¼ teaspoon salt
¼ teaspoon Worcestershire sauce
5 drops Tabasco
   Fine, dry bread crumbs
1 egg, slightly beaten
2 teaspoons water

1. A deep saucepan or an automatic deep-fryer will be needed.
2. Force Camembert cheese and cream cheese through a fine sieve into a heavy 2-qt. saucepan.
3. Blend in milk, flour, butter, salt, Worcestershire sauce, and Tabasco until smooth.
4. Cook over moderate heat, stirring constantly, until mixture is thick and smooth. Cool slightly; cover and chill in refrigerator 6 hrs. or overnight.
5. About 20 min. before deep-frying, fill the saucepan or deep-fryer with fat and heat to 365°F.
6. Shape chilled mixture into balls about ¾ in. in diameter. Roll in bread crumbs.
7. Dip in mixture of egg and water.
8. Roll again in the bread crumbs.
9. Deep-fry cheese balls in heated fat. Fry only as many cheese balls at one time as will float uncrowded one layer deep in fat. Deep-fry 1 to 2 min., or until balls are lightly browned. Lift out with slotted spoon and drain cheese balls over fat for a second before removing to absorbent paper. Insert a wooden pick into each ball; serve immediately.

3½ to 4 doz. cheese balls

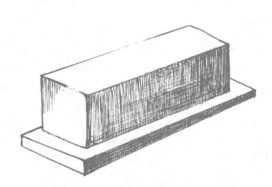

Cheese-Olive Squares

6 slices bread
   Butter or margarine
4 oz. Mozzarella cheese (about 1 cup, shredded)
½ cup finely chopped ripe olives
2 tablespoons chopped pimiento
2 tablespoons grated Parmesan cheese
1 clove garlic, minced; or crushed in a garlic press

1. Toast bread.
2. Spread one side of each slice with butter or margarine.
3. Shred Mozzarella cheese and set aside.
4. Prepare and mix olives and pimiento together in a bowl.
5. Mix in the shredded cheese with Parmesan cheese and garlic.
6. Spread each slice with 3 tablespoons mixture.
7. Set temperature control of range at Broil (500°F or higher).
8. Arrange slices on broiler rack and place in broiler with tops about 3 in. from heat source. Broil 1 to 2 min., or until bubbling hot.
9. To serve, trim crusts off and cut each slice into 4 squares.

2 doz. appetizers

Olive Bites

25 pitted ripe olives
3 tablespoons finely minced green onion
4 oz. sharp Cheddar cheese (about 1 cup, grated)
½ cup sifted all-purpose flour
¼ teaspoon salt
⅛ teaspoon dry mustard
3 tablespoons butter or margarine, melted and slightly cooled
1 teaspoon milk
2 drops Tabasco

1. Set out baking sheet.
2. Set out olives.
3. Stuff olives with onion.
4. Set olives aside.
5. Grate Cheddar cheese.
6. Sift together flour, salt, and dry mustard into a bowl.
7. Mix in the cheese. Stir in a mixture of butter or margarine, milk, and Tabasco.
8. Using about a teaspoon of dough for each, shape dough around olives, completely covering them. Place on baking sheet.
9. Bake at 400°F 10 to 12 min.

25 Olive Bites

Buttermilk Fondue

1 pound Swiss cheese, shredded (about 4 cups)
3 tablespoons cornstarch
½ teaspoon salt
⅛ teaspoon white pepper
¼ teaspoon dry mustard
2 cups buttermilk
1 clove garlic, split in half
1 loaf dark rye bread, cut into 1-inch cubes

1. Toss cheese with a mixture of cornstarch, salt, pepper, and dry mustard. Set aside.
2. In a fondue saucepan, heat buttermilk with garlic over low heat. When hot, remove garlic and add cheese; stir constantly until cheese is melted.
3. Keep fondue warm over low heat while dipping bread cubes.

4 to 6 servings

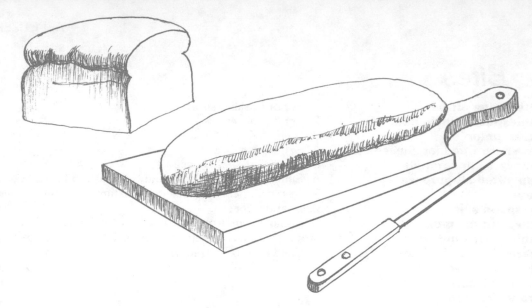

Breads

Cheese Yeast Bread

2¼	cups milk
1	pkg. active dry yeast
¼	cup warm water, 110°F to 115°F (If using compressed yeast, soften 1 cake in ¼ cup lukewarm water, 80°F to 85°F.)
10	oz. sharp Cheddar cheese (about 2½ cups, shredded)
2	tablespoons sugar
1	tablespoon shortening
2	teaspoons salt
1	cup sifted all-purpose flour
5	cups sifted all-purpose flour
	Melted butter or margarine

1. Two 9½ 5¼ x 2¾ in. loaf pans will be needed.
2. Scald milk.
3. Meanwhile, soften yeast in water.
4. Set aside.
5. Shred Cheddar cheese.
6. Set aside.
7. Put sugar, shortening, and salt into a large bowl.
8. Immediately pour scalded milk over ingredients in bowl and stir until shortening is melted. When lukewarm, beat in 1 cup sifted all-purpose flour until smooth.
9. Stir softened yeast and add, mixing well.
10. Measure 4 to 5 cups sifted all-purpose flour.
11. Add about one-half of the flour to yeast mixture and beat until very smooth. Add and mix in the cheese and enough of the remaining flour to make a soft dough. Turn dough onto a lightly floured surface. Let it rest 5 to 10 min.
12. Knead.
13. Form dough into a ball and put it in a greased, deep bowl. Turn dough to bring greased surface to top. Cover with waxed paper and a clean towel and let stand in warm place (about 80ºF) until dough is doubled.
14. Grease loaf pans.
15. Punch down dough with fist and turn out onto a lightly floured surface. Divide dough into two equal portions. Cover and allow to rest 5 to 10 min. Shape each portion into a loaf and put into greased pan. Brush tops of loaves with melted butter or margarine.
16. Cover loaves with waxed paper and towel and let rise again until doubled.
17. Bake at 375ºF about 50 min., or until bread sounds hollow when lightly tapped.

Two loaves bread.

Cheese Tricorn Rolls

1	pkg. active dry yeast
¼	cup warm water, 110°F to 115°F (If using compressed yeast, soften 1 cake in ¼ cup lukewarm water, 80°F to 85°F)
¼	cup warm water
¾	cup sifted all-purpose flour
4	oz. sharp Cheddar cheese (about 1 cup, grated)
¼	cup plus 2 tablespoons shortening
1	tablespoon lemon juice
½	cup sugar
½	teaspoon salt
1	egg
1	egg white
2¼	cups sifted all-purpose flour
	Melted butter or margarine

1. Two baking sheets will be needed.
2. Soften yeast in ¼ cup warm water.
3. Set aside.
4. Meanwhile, pour ¼ cup warm water into a large bowl.
5. Blend in ¾ cup sifted all-purpose flour.
6. Stir softened yeast and add, mixing well. Beat until very smooth. Cover bowl with waxed paper and a clean towel and let stand in warm place (about 80ºF) 1½ to 2 hrs.
7. Meanwhile, grate cheese and set aside.
8. Cream shortening and lemon juice until blended.
9. Add gradually, creaming until fluffy after each addition, a mixture of sugar and salt.
10. Beat egg and egg white until thick.
11. Add beaten eggs in thirds to sugar mixture, beating thoroughly after each addition. Add yeast mixture, mixing well.
12. Measure 2¼ cups sifted all-purpose flour.
13. Add about one-half the flour to yeast mixture and beat until very smooth. Blend in grated cheese, mixing thoroughly. Beat in enough of the remaining flour to make a soft dough. Turn dough onto a lightly floured surface and allow it to rest 5 to 10 min.
14. Knead.
15. Shape dough into a smooth ball and put into a greased deep bowl. Turn dough to bring greased surface to top. Cover with waxed paper and a clean towel and let stand in a warm place (about 80ºF) until dough is doubled.
16. Grease the baking sheets.
17. Punch dough down with fist. Turn out onto a lightly floured surface, cover and allow dough to rest 5 to 10 min.
18. Roll dough ¼ in. thick. Cut into 3-in. squares. Crease each square diagonally across center by pressing with handle of knife or wooden spoon. Fold squares on creases to form triangles; press edges to seal. Place rolls on baking sheets and brush tops with melted butter or margarine.
19. Cover rolls with waxed paper and towel and let rise again until doubled.
20. Bake at 350ºF 40 to 45 min., or until golden brown.

2 doz. tricorn rolls

Maria's Filled Loaf

1	unsliced loaf white bread
2	tablespoons melted butter

Crab Meat Stew

2	tablespoons butter
3	tablespoons flour
1½	cups milk and crab meat liquid
	salt
	pepper
½	teaspoon parsley
12	oz. crab meat
6	tablespoons coarsely grated cheddar cheese

1. Cut off the top part of the bread and remove most of the dough from the lower part. Brush the crust with melted butter inside and out.
2. Heat butter and flour for the stew for a few minutes over low heat. Add milk and crab meat liquid and bring mixture to a boil for a few minutes. Reduce to low heat.
3. Season with salt, pepper, parsley and stir in the crab meat.
4. Fill the loaf with the stew and sprinkle the grated cheese on top. Bake in a 450°F oven for 8-10 minutes until it has turned light brown. Serve with a **green salad** and **lemon wedges.**

Serves 6

No-Knead Cheese Rolls

1½   **cups unsifted all-purpose flour**
1   **pkg. active dry yeast**
3   **tablespoons sugar**
1   **teaspoon salt**
¾   **cup milk**
½   **cup water**
3   **tablespoons butter or margarine**
1   **cup unsifted all-purpose flour**
4   **oz. sharp Cheddar cheese (about 1 cup, grated)**
¼   **cup butter or margarine**
1   **egg yolk**
1   **tablespoon milk**

1. Combine 1½ cups unsifted all-purpose flour, yeast, sugar, and salt in a large mixer bowl and blend thoroughly.
2. Measure ¾ cup milk, water, and butter or margarine into a saucepan and heat until liquids are warm. (It is not necessary for the shortening to be entirely melted.)
3. Gradually add liquids to the dry ingredients in mixer bowl, beating for 2 min. at medium speed of electric mixer, scraping the bowl occasionally.
4. Add and beat 1 cup unsifted all-purpose flour at high speed 2 min., scraping the bowl occasionally.
5. Mix in enough additional flour (½ to 1 cup, unsifted) to make a soft dough. (Dough will be slightly sticky.)
6. Put the dough into a greased deep bowl. Cover with waxed paper and a clean towel and let stand in a warm place (about 80°F) until dough is doubled, 45 to 60 min.
7. Generously grease baking sheets.
8. Grate Cheddar cheese, cover to prevent drying, and set aside.
9. Melt butter or margarine and set aside.
10. Punch down dough with fist and turn dough out onto a lightly floured surface. Divide dough into two equal portions. Set one portion aside. Roll dough into a rectangle 16x8 in. Brush with about one-half of melted butter. Sprinkle with about one-half of grated cheese. Cut crosswise into 8 equal portions. Cut into halves lengthwise. Fold each strip in thirds, lapping each side portion over center third. Place rolls on baking sheet. Repeat for other half of dough.
11. Beat yolk and 1 tablespoon milk slightly.
12. Brush tops of rolls with egg yolk mixture. Let rise until doubled, about 30 min.
13. Bake at 425°F about 8 min., or until rolls are golden brown.
14. Serve rolls hot.

About 2½ doz. rolls

Date-Nut Cheese Bread

½   **lb. pitted dates (about 1½ cups, cut)**
¾   **cup very hot water**
¼   **cup shortening**
3   **cups sifted all-purpose flour**
½   **cup sugar**
4   **teaspoons baking powder**
¾   **teaspoon salt**
1   **cup (about 4 oz.) grated sharp Cheddar cheese**
¾   **cup (about 3 oz.) chopped pecans**
½   **cup milk**
1   **egg, well beaten**
1   **teaspoon vanilla extract**

1. Grease bottom of a 9½x5¼x2¾-in. loaf pan.
2. Cut dates finely and put them into a bowl.
3. Pour hot water over dates.
4. Set aside to cool.
5. Melt shortening and set aside to cool.
6. Sift flour, sugar, baking powder, and salt together into a bowl.
7. Prepare and lightly blend Cheddar cheese and pecans into dry ingredients.
8. Add to the date-water mixture the cooled shortening, milk, egg, and vanilla extract.
9. Mix well. Make a well in center of dry ingredients and add date-liquid mixture all at one time. Stir only enough to moisten dry ingredients. Turn mixture into pan and spread to corners.
10. Bake at 350°F about 65 min., or until bread is done. Remove from pan and cool.

1 loaf bread

Puff-Pastry Cheese Twists

1 **cup butter**
2 **cups sifted all-purpose flour**
½ **teaspoon salt**
7 **tablespoons iced water**
2 **oz. Parmesan cheese (about ½ cup, grated)**
Egg white, beaten
¼ **teaspoon paprika**
¼ **teaspoon salt**

1. *For Puff Pastry* — Put butter into a large bowl of cold water and ice cubes or chipped ice.
2. Work butter with hands. Break it into small portions and squeeze each in water about 20 times, or until butter is pliable and waxy. Remove butter and wipe off excess water. Reserve ¼ cup of this butter and set it in the refrigerator. Quickly pat remainder ½ in. thick, divide into 5 equal portions, wrap each in waxed paper. Set in refrigerator to keep it thoroughly chilled.
3. Sift flour and salt together into a bowl.
4. With two knives or pastry blender, cut in the reserved ¼ cup butter until pieces are the size of small peas. Sprinkle iced water gradually over mixture, 1 tablespoon at a time.
5. Mix lightly with a fork after each addition. When blended, gather into a ball and knead. Cover with a bowl and allow dough to rest about 30 min.
6. Roll dough on floured surface to form rectangle ¼ in. thick. Keep corners square, gently pulling dough into shape where necessary.
7. Remove one portion of the chilled butter and cut into small pieces. Quickly pat pieces down center third of dough. Cover the butter with right-hand third of dough. Fold left-hand third under butter section. With rolling pin, gently press down and seal open edges. Wrap pastry in waxed paper. Chill in refrigerator about 1 hr.
8. Remove from refrigerator and place on the board with butter section near top, narrow side toward you. Turn folded dough one-quarter way around, under-open edge away from you. Roll to original size. Dot with a second portion of butter, fold, wrap and chill about 1 hr. Using third, fourth and fifth portions of butter, repeat entire procedure three times. Each time, place dough on floured surface as directed, roll, wrap and chill.
9. With the last rolling, fold four sides toward center. Gently press down with rolling pin. Fold in half. Wrap dough in waxed paper. Cover with a damp towel and place in refrigerator. Chill in refrigerator 2 hrs. before using.
10. To store for several days, wrap dough in waxed paper and set in refrigerator.
11. *For Cheese Twists* — Lightly grease two baking sheets.
12. Grate Parmesan cheese.
13. Set aside.
14. Divide the dough into 2 equal portions. Return one portion to refrigerator while rolling out the other portion. Roll dough into a rectangle 13½x12 in. Brush dough with egg white.
15. Sprinkle evenly over surface one half of the grated Parmesan cheese and one half of a mixture of paprika and salt.
16. Cut rectangle into halves to make two 13½x6-in. pieces. Cut each half into strips 6x1½ in. Twist each strip. Arrange the strips on one of the greased baking sheets. Set in refrigerator for 15 min. Repeat procedure, using the remaining Parmesan cheese and seasonings with the remaining portion of dough.
17. Bake at 400°F 15 min. Reduce heat to 300°F and bake about 10 min. longer, or until twists are golden brown.

3 doz. cheese twists

Cheese Fans

4   oz. sharp Cheddar cheese
(about 1 cup, grated)
2   cups sifted all-purpose
flour
1   tablespoon baking powder
1   teaspoon salt
½   cup lard, hydrogenated
vegetable shortening or
all-purpose shortening
½   cup milk
Softened butter
Melted butter

1. Grease bottoms of 12 2½-in. muffin pan wells.
2. Grate Cheddar cheese and set aside.
3. Sift together flour, baking powder, and salt into a bowl.
4. Cut lard, hydrogenated vegetable shortening or all-purpose shortening into dry ingredients with a pastry blender or two knives until mixture resembles coarse corn meal.
5. Make a well in center of mixture and add milk all at one time.
6. Stir with fork until dough follows fork.
7. Gently form dough into a ball and put on a lightly floured surface. Knead it lightly with finger tips 10 to 15 times. Roll dough into a 12x10-in. rectangle about ¼ in. thick. Cut into 5 strips. Spread with softened butter.
8. Sprinkle four strips with the grated cheese. Stack the four strips and top with the fifth strip. Cut into 12 equal sections. Place on end in muffin pan wells. Brush tops with melted butter.
9. Bake at 450°F 10 to 15 min., or until biscuits are golden brown.
10 Serve with hot butter.

1 doz. Cheese Fans

Cheese Biscuits: Follow recipe for Cheese Fans. Reduce cheese to ¾ cup, grated, and add with the shortening. Roll dough to ½-in. thickness, keeping thickness uniform. Cut with a floured biscuit cutter, using an even pressure to keep sides of biscuits straight. Place on a greased baking sheet, close together for soft-sided biscuits, or 1 in. apart for crusty sides.

Tender Cheese Biscuit Ring: Follow recipe for Cheese Fans. Increase recipe one and one-half times. Roll dough into a rectangle ½ in. thick and 8 in. wide. Spread with 2 tablespoons softened **butter.** Sprinkle the grated cheese evenly over the dough. Starting at the longer side of dough, roll up and pinch edge to seal (do not pinch ends of roll). Place roll on greased baking sheet, sealed edge down. Bring ends of roll together to form a ring. Brush with 1 tablespoon melted butter. With scissors or knife, cut at 1½-in. intervals through ring to ¼ in. from center. Turn each section on its side. Bake at 400°F 20 to 25 mi;n., or until ring is light golden brown. Serve immediately with **butter.**

Swiss Cheese Pancakes

6   oz. Swiss cheese (about
1½ cups, grated)
¾   cup thick sour cream
3   egg yolks, slightly beaten
2   tablespoons plus 1 teaspoon all-purpose flour
¾   teaspoon salt
1½ teaspoons thyme
½   teaspoon dry mustard
2   tablespoons butter

1. Set out a heavy skillet.
2. Grate Swiss cheese.
3. Add sour cream and egg yolks to cheese, mixing well after each addition and a mixture of flour, salt, thyme, and dry mustard.
4. Melt butter in the skillet over low heat.
5. Drop batter by teaspoonfuls into skillet. Cook over medium heat until lightly browned on bottom. Loosen edges with a spatula, turn and lightly brown other side.
6. Serve at once with bacon or pork sausage.

About 2 doz. 3-in. pancakes

Special Cheese Waffles

⅓ cup butter or margarine
½ lb. sharp Cheddar cheese
 (about 2 cups, shredded)
1¾ cups sifted all-purpose
 flour
1½ tablespoons sugar
1 tablespoon baking powder
¾ teaspoon salt
2 egg yolks
1¼ cups milk
2 egg whites

1. Heat waffle baker while preparing batter.
2. Melt butter or margarine and set aside to cool.
3. Shred Cheddar cheese and set aside.
4. Sift together flour, sugar, baking powder, and salt into a bowl and set aside.
5. Beat egg yolks until thick and lemon-colored.
6. Blend in the cooled shortening, cheese and milk.
7. Add liquid mixture all at one time to dry ingredients; mix only until batter is blended.
8. Beat egg whites until rounded peaks are formed.
9. Spread egg whites over batter and gently fold together.
10. Unless temperature is automatically shown on waffle baker, test heat by dropping a few drops of water on grids. It is hot enough for baking when the drops of water sputter.
11. Pour batter into center of waffle grids. It is wise to experiment to find out the exact amount of batter your baker will hold; use that same measurement (spoonfuls or cupfuls) in future waffle baking.
12. Lower cover and allow waffle to bake according to manufacturer's directions, or until steaming stops (4 to 5 min.). Do not raise cover during baking period; then lift carefully and loosen waffle with a fork.
13. Serve immediately with butter or margarine and maple syrup, accompanied with sausage links or bacon. Cheese waffles may also be served topped with creamed eggs, fish, chicken or vegetables.

4 9-in. square waffles

Cheese-Nut Waffles: Follow recipe for Special Cheese Waffles. Fold ½ cup (2 oz.) chopped **nuts** into batter with the egg whites.

Bacon-Cheese Waffles: Follow recipe for Special Cheese Waffles. Panbroil 8 slices **bacon** until crisp; crumble and fold into batter with the egg whites.

Golden Spoon Bread

6   oz. sharp Cheddar cheese
     (about 1½ cups, grated)
2   cups milk
4   egg yolks
1   cup yellow corn meal
¼   cup butter
1   teaspoon sugar
½   teaspoon salt
4   egg whites

1. Thoroughly grease a 1½-qt. casserole.
2. Shred or grate Cheddar cheese and set aside.
3. Scald milk in top of double broiler.
4. Meanwhile, beat egg yolks until thick and lemon-colored.
5. Set aside.
6. When milk is scalded, add corn meal very gradually, stirring constantly.
7. Stir until mixture thickens and becomes smooth. Remove double boiler top from simmering water. Gradually add the beaten egg yolks, stirring constantly; then mix in the grated cheese, butter, sugar, and salt.
8. Beat egg whites until rounded peaks are formed.
9. Gently spread beaten egg whites over corn meal mixture; carefully fold together until just blended. Turn mixture into casserole.
10. Bake at 375°F 35 to 40 min., or until a wooden pick or cake tester comes out clean when inserted at the center.
11. Serve piping hot with butter and maple syrup or honey.

6 to 8 servings

Mozzarella Egg Bread

7   to 8 cups all-purpose flour
2   packages acitve dry yeast
1   tablespoon sugar
1   tablespoon salt
6   eggs (at room
     temperature)
1   cup plain yogurt
2   cups shredded mozzarella
     cheese (8 ounces)
½   cup hot tap water (120°
     to 130°F)

1. Combine 2 cups flour, yeast, sugar, and salt in a mixing bowl.
2. Stir eggs, yogurt, 1½ cups cheese, and water into flour mixture; beat until smooth, about 3 min on high speed of electric mixer.
3. Stir in enough more flour to make a soft dough.
4. Turn dough onto a floured surface; knead until smooth and elastic (5 to 8 minutes).
5. Place in an oiled bowl; turn to oil top of dough. Cover; let rise in a warm place until double in bulk (about 1 hour).
6. Punch dough down. Divide in half; shape into loaves, and place in 2 greased 9x5x3-inch loaf pans. Cover; let rise until double, about 30 minutes. Top loaves with remaining cheese.
7. Bake at 375°F 30 minutes, or until done.

2 loaves

Pizza

Dough
1   oz. yeast
½   teaspoon salt
2   tablespoons salad oil
½   cup warm water
1½   cups flour

Filling
1   lb. ground beef
3   tomatoes, sliced
1   teaspoon tarragon, or
     oregano
6   slices mozzarella cheese
½   cup Parmesan cheese,
     grated
1   can anchovy fillets (op-
     tional)

1. Crumble yeast in bowl and stir it with ½ teaspoon salt and 2 tablespoons oil. Add ½ cup warm water so that yeast dissolves thoroughly.
2. Mix in the flour and work the dough together. Set aside to rise for 30 minutes.
3. Roll out the dough and place on a cookie sheet.
4. Spread the ground beef on the dough and arrange the sliced tomatoes on top. Sprinkle with tarragon.
5. Put cheese slices on top of the tomatoes and sprinkle on a thick layer of the grated cheese. Anchovy fillets can also be put on the tomatoes before the cheese is added. Bake in a 450°F oven for 15-20 minutes until the cheese is melted, and the meat brown.

Serves 4

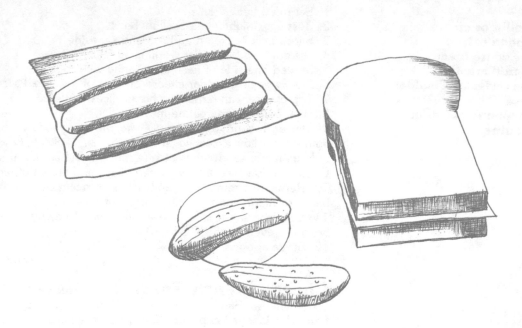

Sandwiches & Fillings

Hot 'n' Hearty
Cheese-Plus Sandwiches

Prepare sandwiches. Set temperature control of range at Broil (500°F or higher). Arrange sandwiches on broiler rack and put into broiler with tops of sandwiches 3 in. below source of heat. Broil until cheese is melted and other ingredients are thoroughly heated. Serve sandwiches hot.

Open-Face Frankfurter — Spread **bread** with **prepare mustard.** Slice a **frankfurter** in thirds lengthwise and place over the mustard. Top with 1 slice **Cheddar cheese,** 1 slice **tomato,** 1 slice **stuffed olive** and an **onion ring.**

Broiled Bean — Spread **bread** with **ketchup** or **chili sauce.** Generously cover with **baked beans.** Top with 1 slice **Cheddar cheese,** 1 thin slice **Bermuda onion** and 1 slice **stuffed olive.**

Triple Pickle — Sprinkle **bread** with a mixture of crumbled crisp **bacon** and finely chopped **onion.**

Cover with 1 slice **Brick cheese.** Slice **dill pickle** crosswise and arrange 3 slices on top of cheese.

Liver Sausage — Generously spread **bread** with **butter,** then with **prepared horse-radish.** Mash **liver sausage** and spread evenly to edges of bread. Top with 2 or 3 **sweet onion slices** and 1 slice **Cheddar cheese.**

Crossed Bacon — Spread **bread** with **butter.** Cover with 1 slice **"boiled" ham,** 1 or more slices **tomato,** 1 slice process **Cheddar cheese,** and 2 slices partially cooked **bacon,** crossed diagonally.

Toasted Cheese — Toast one side of **bread slices** in broiler; watch carefully to avoid scorching. Remove from broiler and spread untoasted sides with **butter.** Cover each slice with **Cheddar cheese.** Return to broiler. Broil until cheese bubbles and is melted. If desired, top each with a thin slice of **tomato,** or sprinkle lightly with **sugar.**

French Toast-Cheese Sandwiches

2	eggs
1/3	cup milk or cream
1/2	teaspoon salt
8	slices white bread
	Prepared mustard
4	slices Swiss or Cheddar cheese
3	tablespoons butter or margarine

1. Set out a heavy skillet.
2. Beat eggs slightly in a shallow bowl.
3. Stir in milk or cream and salt and set aside.
4. Set out bread on a flat working surface.
5. Spread one side of each slice lightly with mustard.
6. Put Swiss or Cheddar cheese on four of the bread slices.
7. Top cheese with remaining bread slices, buttered side down.
8. Heat butter or margarine in the skillet.
9. Dip each sandwich carefully into the egg mixture, coating both sides. Allow excess egg mixture to drain back into bowl. Dip only as many sandwiches at one time as will lie flat in skillet. Cook over low heat until browned. Turn and brown other side.
10. Repeat for remaining sandwiches. If necessary, add more butter or margarine to skillet to prevent sticking.
11. Or place sandwiches on a well-greased baking sheet and brown in oven at 450°F 8 to 10 min.
12. Serve at once.

4 sandwiches

Cheese French Toast: Follow recipe for French Toast-Cheese Sandwiches. Shred 4 oz. **Swiss cheese** or **Cheddar** (about 1 cup, shredded). Add cheese to egg mixture, beating well. Omit mustard and Swiss cheese slices. Spread slices with egg-cheese mixture and fry.

Savory Cheese Sandwiches

8	oz. Cheddar cheese (about 2 cups, shredded)
1	egg
2	tablespoons butter
1	tablespoon chopped onion
1	tablespoon all-purpose flour
1/2	cup cream
1/4	teaspoon salt
2	drops Tabasco
2	tablespoons lemon juice
1	tablespoon chopped pimiento
1	tablespoon chopped stuffed olives
12	slices bacon
6	slices bread
	Butter, softened

1. Shred Cheddar cheese and set aside.
2. Hard-cook egg, chop and set aside.
3. Melt butter in a skillet over low heat.
4. Add and cook onion until transparent.
5. Add and stir flour until blended.
6. Heat until mixture bubbles. Remove from heat.
7. Add cream, salt, and Tabasco gradually while stirring constantly.
8. Cook until mixture boils. Cook 1 to 2 min. longer. Remove from heat. Blend in lemon juice.
9. Add to the cream mixture the cheese, egg, pimiento, and stuffed olives.
10. Mix well and set aside.
11. Panbroil bacon until partially cooked.
12. Spread bread with softened butter.
13. Spread cheese mixture on the bread, allowing 1/4 cup for each slice. Top each with 2 of the bacon slices, crossed diagonally.
14. Set temperature control of range at Broil (500°F or higher). Arrange sandwiches on broiler rack and place in broiler with tops of sandwiches 3 in. below source of heat. Broil until cheese mixture is bubbly and slightly browned and bacon slices are crisp.
15. Serve hot.

6 open-face sandwiches

Glamorous Triple Decker Sandwich

3   slices French toast (see
    Cheese French Toast
    recipe, page 32; omit
    cheese)
1   slice Swiss cheese
1   slice cooked ham
½   teaspoon dry mustard
1   teaspoon water
    Sliced cooked chicken

1. Prepare French toast.
2. *To Assemble Sandwich*—Place on top of one slice French toast 1 slice Swiss cheese and 1 slice cooked ham.
3. Top with second French toast slice.
4. Spread with a mixture of dry mustard and water.
5. Place chicken on Mustard mixture.
6. Top with remaining French toast slice.

1 sandwich

Cheese-Stuffed Franks in Buns

12 frankfurters
½   cup sweet pickle relish
1   tablespoon prepared
    mustard
¾   lb. process Cheddar
    cheese
12 slices bacon
12 buns, buttered and toasted

1. Slit frankfurters almost through lengthwise.
2. Mix together pickle relish and prepared mustard.
3. Cut Cheddar cheese into 12 4x½x½-in. strips.
4. Put one strip of cheese and about 2 teaspoons of the relish mixture into each frankfurter and set aside.
5. Panbroil bacon until partially cooked.
6. Drain. Starting at one end, wrap one slice of bacon around each frankfurter; secure each end with a wooden pick.
7. Set temperature control of range at Broil (500°F or higher). Arrange the bacon-wrapped frankfurters on the broiler rack with tops 3 in. below source of heat and broil until bacon is cooked, turning once.
8. Serve in buns.

6 servings

Broiled Cheese-Olive Sandwiches

2   eggs
½   lb. sharp Cheddar cheese
      (about 2 cups, grated)
1¼   cups chopped, pitted ripe
      olives
½   cup chopped green pepper
¼   cup chopped onion
⅓   cup ketchup
2   tablespoons mayonnaise
      or salad dressing
2   teaspoons prepared
      mustard
¼   teaspoon marjoram
⅛   teaspoon oregano
⅛   teaspoon salt
      Few grains pepper
4   sandwich buns
      Butter or margarine

1. Hard-cook eggs and slice into a medium-size bowl.
2. Grate Cheddar cheese and put into the bowl.
3. Prepare and add olives, green pepper, and onion.
4. Blend together ketchup, mayonnaise or salad dressing, and prepared mustard and a mixture of marjoram, oregano, salt, and pepper.
5. Add to mixture in bowl and blend. Set aside.
6. Set temperature control of range at Broil (500°F or higher).
7. Split buns with a sharp knife.
8. Set buns on broiler rack, cut sides up, and place broiler rack in broiler with tops of buns 2 in. from heat source. Toast until buns are golden brown. Remove broiler rack from broiler and spread toasted sides of buns with butter or margarine.
9. Spread about ⅛ of cheese mixture on buttered side of each bun. Return broiler rack to broiler with tops of sandwiches 3 in. from heat source. Broil until cheese is bubbly.
10. Serve immediately.

8 sandwiches

Taste-Teaser Tuna Sandwiches

1   cup (7-oz. can, drained)
     flaked tuna
8   slices crisp panbroiled
     bacon, crumbled
¼   cup chopped celery
2   tablespoons chopped
     chives
2   tablespoons chopped
     green pepper
3   tablespoons mayonnaise
⅛   teaspoon freshly ground
     pepper
8   slices white or whole
     wheat bread
     Prepared mustard
     Process cheese spread
     with pimiento
3   eggs, well beaten
1½   cups milk
¾   teaspoon salt
     Sprigs of parsley
     Sprinkling of paprika

1. *For Tuna Filling (About 2 cups filling)*—Mix tuna, bacon, celery, chives, green pepper, mayonnaise, and ground pepper thoroughly and set aside.
2. *For Sandwiches*—Lightly grease an 8x8x2-in. baking dish.
3. Arrange bread in two stacks on a flat working surface.
4. With a sharp knife, trim crusts from slices. Spread one side of each slice with prepared mustard.
5. Spread four slices of bread, mustard side up, with the Tuna Filling. Place in baking dish. Top filling with remaining bread slices, placing them mustard side down.
6. Spread Process cheese spread with pimiento lavishly over each sandwich.
7. Set aside.
8. Blend eggs, milk, and salt thoroughly.
9. Pour the egg mixture over the sandwiches.
10. Bake at 325°F 40 min., or until golden brown.
11. Serve sandwiches hot, garnished with parsley and paprika.
12. Accompany with relishes such as **carrot curls** and **radish fans.**

4 sandwiches

Olive and Pecan Filling

3   oz. (1 pkg.) cream cheese
2   tablespoons milk
2   drops Tabasco
     Few grains salt
⅓   cup chopped green olives
¼   cup (about 1 oz.) chopped
     salted pecans

1. Beat cream cheese until fluffy.
2. Blend in milk, Tabasco, and salt.
3. Finely chop olives and pecans.
4. Blend into cream cheese mixture.

Enough filling for 4 sandwiches

Bacon-Cottage Cheese Filling

4   slices bacon
1   cup cream-style cottage
     cheese
2   teaspoons mayonnaise
2   tablespoons chopped
     sweet pickle
½   teaspoon grated onion
     Few grains paprika

1. Dice bacon and panbroil until crisp.
2. Thoroughly blend together cottage cheese and mayonnaise.
3. Mix in lightly but thoroughly the bacon, pickle, onion, and paprika.

Enough filling for 4 sandwiches.

Frosted Sandwich Treats

1⅓   **cups (6½-oz. can) drained crab meat, bony tissue removed**

¼   **cup mayonnaise**

2   **tablespoons ketchup**

1   **tablespoon lemon juice**

½   **teaspoon Worcestershire sauce**

¼   **teaspoon salt**

⅛   **teaspoon pepper**

¾   **cup (about 4 oz.) toasted almonds, finely chopped**

½   **cup (about 3 oz.) chopped stuffed olives**

2   **tablespoons mayonnaise**

1   **teaspoon prepared mustard**

16   **oz. cream cheese, softened**

⅔   **cup (about 1 small) grated cucumber**

¼   **teaspoon finely chopped chives**

⅛   **teaspoon onion salt**

⅛   **teaspoon salt**

⅛   **teaspoon pepper**

1   **cup (about 1 large) sieved avocado**

¼   **cup (about 1 oz.) crumbled Roquefort or Blue cheese**

1   **teaspoon lemon juice**

¼   **teaspoon garlic salt**

2   **cups (about ½ lb.) ground cooked ham**

¼   **cup minced parsley**

2   **tablespoons thick sour cream**

2   **tablespoons prepared horse-radish**

3   **tablespoons orange juice**

2   **drops yellow food coloring**

1   **cup butter or margarine**

42   **slices thin-sliced white bread**

1. *For Crab-Meat Spread*—Blend together crab meat, mayonnaise, ketchup, lemon juice, Worcestershire sauce, salt, and pepper.
2. Put in refrigerator until ready to use.
3. *For Almond-Olive Spread*—Blend together almonds, olives, mayonnaise, and prepared mustard.
4. Put in refrigerator until ready to use.
5. *For Cucumber Spread*—Beat cream cheese, cucumber, chives, onion salt, salt, and pepper until fluffy.
6. Put in refrigerator until ready to use.
7. *For Avocado Spread*—Blend together avocado, Roquefort or Blue cheese, lemon juice, and garlic salt.
8. Put in refrigerator until ready to use.
9. *For Ham and Horse-radish Spread*—Blend together ham, parsley, sour cream, and horse-radish.
10. Put in refrigerator until ready to use.
11. *For Frosting*—Beat together cream cheese, orange juice, and food coloring until fluffy.
12. Cover and set aside.
13. *For Sandwiches*—Whip butter or margarine at high speed with electric mixer.
14. Arrange white bread in several stacks on a flat working surface.
15. With a sharp knife, trim off crusts. Spread each slice with the whipped butter. Spread 7 of the bread slices with Crab-Meat Spread, 7 with Almond-Olive Spread, 7 with Ham and Horse-radish Spread, 7 with Cucumber Spread, and 7 with Avocado Spread.
16. Arrange these slices in 7 stacks, all 5 different fillings in each stack. Top each stack with one of the 7 remaining bread slices, buttered side down. Cut each stack diagonally into halves. Spread top and one side of each triangular stack with the cream cheese "Frosting."
17. Garnish each triangle with one of the following impaled on a cocktail pick: pimiento-stuffed **olive,** small cooked **shrimp,** pickled **onion** or rolled **anchovy fillet.**
18. Arrange on serving platter. Garnish with radish roses and parsley.

14 servings

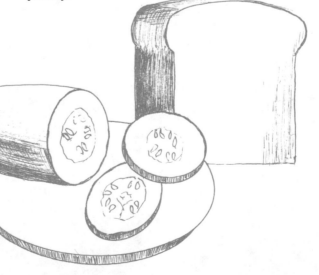

Party Sandwich Loaf

8 slices crisp panbroiled bacon, crumbled
1 cup finely chopped, cooked chicken
¼ cup mayonnaise
1 tablespoon finely chopped pimiento
¼ teaspoon salt
⅛ teaspoon pepper
11 oz. (1 pkg.) cream cheese, softened
1 cup (about 4 oz.) finely chopped toasted pecans
¾ cup (8¼-oz. can) well-drained crushed pineapple (reserve syrup for "Frosting" of loaf)
1 hard-cooked egg, chopped
1⅓ cups (7-oz. can) finely chopped shrimp
¼ cup finely chopped celery
¼ cup chili sauce
2 tablespoons lemon juice
¼ teaspoon salt
Few grains pepper
2 drops red food coloring
½ cup butter or margarine
1 unsliced loaf sandwich bread
Minced parsley
Stuffed olive slices

1. *For Chicken-Bacon Filling*—Blend bacon, chicken, mayonnaise, pimiento and a mixture of salt, and pepper.
2. Put in refrigerator until ready to use.
3. *For Toasted Pecan Filling*—Blend together cream cheese, pecans, and pineapple.
4. Put in refrigerator until ready to use.
5. *For Shrimp Salad Filling*—Blend together egg, shrimp, celery, chili sauce, lemon juice, salt, and pepper.
6. Put in refrigerator until ready to use.
7. *For "Frosting"*—Beat together until fluffy the reserved pineapple syrup, cream cheese, and food coloring.
8. Cover and set aside.
9. *For Sandwich Loaf*—Whip butter or margarine at high speed of electric mixer .
10. Trim crust from sandwich bread.
11. Cut the loaf into four equal lengthwise slices. Flatten each slightly with a rolling pin.
12. Spread one side of each slice with the whipped butter or margarine. Place one bread slice, buttered side up, on a serving platter. Spread evenly with Shrimp Salad Filling. Top with second bread slice and spread evenly with Toasted Pecan Filling. Top with third bread slice and spread evenly with Chicken-Bacon Filling. Top with remaining bread slice.
13. Frost sides and top of loaf with the "Frosting."
14. Garnish top of loaf with parsley and olive slices.
15. Set loaf ;in refrigerator to chill about 1 hr. before serving.
16. Garnish with crisp **greens** or decorate platter with huckleberry leaves. To serve, cut loaf into slices.

8 to 10 servings

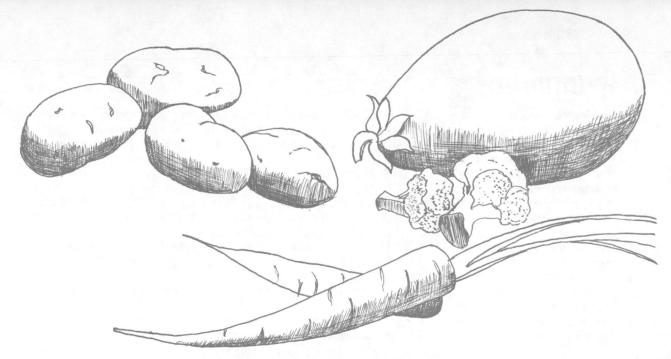

Main Dishes

Chicken Tetrazzini

1	(3 lb) broiler chicken
2	cups water
1	cup dry white wine
2	carrots, cubed
1	medium finely chopped onion
2	parsley stalks
½	teaspoon thyme
1½	teaspoons salt
4	tablespoons butter
5	tablespoons flour
3	cups chicken stock
4	oz. light cream
6	oz. grated Parmesan cheese
1	cup sliced mushrooms
8	oz. ribbon macaroni

1. Place chicken in a casserole. Add water, wine, carrots, onion, parsley, thyme and salt. Bring to a boil, skim and let boil gently for about 40 minutes with casserole covered.
2. Strain the stock and save.
3. Skin and bone the chicken when cold. Cut the meat in slices.
4. Melt 3 tablespoons butter in a saucepan. Add the flour and stir. Add in turns 3 cups stock. Add the cream and heat for about 5 minutes. Stir in the Parmesan cheese, but save some for the top.
5. Preheat the oven to 350°F.
6. Melt the rest of the butter in a frying pan and brown the mushrooms lightly.
7. Bring 2 qts. of water with 3 teaspoons salt to a boil. Add the ribbon macaroni and boil until just soft, but no more.
8. Wash the macaroni and drain.
9. Mix mushrooms and macaroni and place at the bottom of a large ovenproof dish. Put the chicken on top. Pour on the sauce. Sprinkle with the remaining cheese.
10. Bake in the oven for about 15 minutes.

Serves 6

Peasant Omelette

4-5	slices thick bacon
4	boiled potatoes
1	onion
4	eggs
4	tablespoons milk
	salt & pepper
2	tomatoes, sliced
2	oz. Swiss cheese, grated parsley

1. Chop the onion and cut the potatoes in cubes.
2. Brown the bacon, potatoes, and onion in a skillet.
3. Beat the eggs with milk. Add salt and pepper to taste and pour over the ingredients in the skillet.
4. Put sliced tomatoes on top and sprinkle with cheese. Make sure eggs are evenly distributed in the skillet. Cook until omelette is creamy on the surface. About 10 minutes.
5. Serve with **cut parsley** on top.

Beef Italiano

8	slices cooked beef, cut about ⅛ in. thick
⅓	cup fine, dry bread crumbs (about 1 slice bread)
¼	cup (about 1 oz.) grated Parmesan cheese
1	egg, well beaten
2	tablespoons milk
1	teaspoon salt
1	teaspoon dry mustard
⅛	teaspoon pepper
¼	cup shortening
8	slices (8 oz.) process American cheese
1	6-oz. can (¾ cup) tomato paste

1. Thinly slice enough cooked beef to yield 8 slices cooked beef.
2. Mix together bread crumbs and Parmesan cheese.
3. Mix together egg, milk, salt, dry mustard, and pepper in a bowl.
4. Heat shortening in a skillet.
5. Dip beef slices (coat both sides) into the egg mixture. Allow excess egg mixture to drain back into bowl. Dip into crumb mix, coating both sides. Dip only as many slices at one time as will lie flat in skillet. Put into skillet and brown over low heat. Turn and brown other side. Repeat procedure for remaining slices. If necessary, add more shortening to skillet to prevent meat from sticking.
6. Return all slices to skillet. Arrange American cheese over the meat.
7. Pour tomato paste over cheese.
8. Cover and cook over low heat about 15 min.

4 servings

Layered Meat Loaf

1	lb. ground beef
½	lb. bulk pork sausage
1	cup fine, dry bread crumbs
½	cup (about 2 oz.) grated Parmesan cheese
¼	cup finely chopped parsley
½	cup milk
1	egg, beaten
2	teaspoons salt
¼	teaspoon pepper
¾	lb. (about 1½ cups) Ricotta cheese
1	egg, beaten
1	tablespoon chopped chives

1. Grease a 9½x5¼x2¾-in. loaf pan.
2. Lightly mix together ground beef, pork sausage, bread crumbs, Parmesan cheese, onion, parsley, milk, and egg and a mixture of salt and pepper.
3. Lightly pack one half of mixture into loaf pan. Thoroughly blend Ricotta cheese, egg, and chives together and spread over meat in pan.
4. Top with remaining meat mixture, smoothing evenly to corners.
5. Bake at 350°F about 1½ hrs.

About 6 servings

Mozzarella-Layered Meat Loaf: Follow recipe for Layered Meat Loaf. Omit Ricotta cheese mixture. Hard-cook **4 eggs.** Slice and arrange over meat mixture in pan. Cover with 6 slices (3 oz.) **Mozzarella cheese.** Proceed as in recipe.

Veal Parmesan

Tomato Meat Sauce (one-half recipe, page 50)

2 lbs. veal round steak (cutlet), cut about ½ in. thick

1⅓ cups fine, dry bread crumbs (about 4 slices bread)

⅓ cup grated Parmesan cheese

3 eggs, beaten

1 teaspoon salt

¼ teaspoon pepper

⅓ cup olive oil

6 slices (3 oz.) Mozzarella cheese (1 slice per piece)

1. Set out an 11x7x1½-in. baking dish.
2. Prepare sauce (allowing about 4½ hrs.).
3. When sauce is partially done, wipe veal round steak with a clean damp cloth.
4. To increase tenderness, place meat on a flat working surface and repeatedly pound meat on one side with meat hammer. Turn meat and repeat process. Cut into six serving-size pieces. Set aside.
5. Mix together bread crumbs and Parmesan cheese and set aside.
6. Mix together eggs, salt, and pepper.
7. Heat olive oil in a skillet.
8. Dip meat pieces (coat both sides) into egg mixture. Allow excess egg mixture to drain back into bowl. Dip piece into crumb mixture (coat both sides). Dip only as many pieces at one time as will lie flat in skillet. Put in skillet and brown on both sides over low heat.
9. Repeat procedure for remaining pieces. If necessary, add more oil to skillet to prevent sticking. Arrange browned pieces in baking dish. Pour the Tomato-Meat Sauce over them. Top with Mozzarella cheese.
10. Bake at 350°F 15 to 20 min., or until cheese is melted and lightly browned.

6 servings

Light Veal Parmesan: Follow recipe for Veal Parmesan. Brown veal lightly and place in baking dish. Pour over it ¼ cup melted **butter;** sprinkle with ¼ cup grated **Parmesan cheese.** Omit tomato sauce and Mozzarella cheese.

Swiss Cheese Fondue

1 1-lb. loaf French or Italian bread

1 lb. natural Swiss cheese (about 4 cups, shredded)

5 teaspoons cornstarch

2 tablespoons kirsch

1 clove garlic, cut into halves

¼ teaspoon salt

⅛ teaspoon pepper

2 cups Neuchatel or sauterne

1. Set out a chafing dish or 2-qt. top-of-range casserole.
2. Cut French or Italian bread into bite-sized pieces having at least one crusty side, and set aside.
3. Shred Swiss cheese.
4. Mix cornstarch and kirsch together in a small bowl and set aside.
5. Rub the casserole with cut surface of garlic.
6. Put into the casserole the shredded cheese and a mixture of salt and pepper.
7. Pour Neuchatel or sauterne over the cheese.
8. Stirring constantly, cook over medium heat until cheese is melted. Blend in the cornstarch mixture. Continue stirring while cooking 2 to 3 min., or until fondue begins to bubble. Keep the fondue gently bubbling throughout serving time. Serve at the table. Spear bread cubes with a fork; dunk and twirl them in the fondue.

6 to 8 servings

Lasagne

Tomato Meat Sauce
(page 50)
2 eggs
6 qts. water
2 tablespoons salt
1 tablespoon olive oil
1 lb. lasagne noodles
3 tablespoons olive oil
1 lb. ground beef
¾ lb. Mozzarella cheese,
sliced
1 cup (about ½ lb.) Ricotta
cheese
¼ cup (about 1 oz.) grated
Parmesan cheese
½ teaspoon pepper

1. Set out an 8x8x2-in. baking dish.
2. Prepare sauce (allowing about 4½ hrs.).
3. Hard-cook eggs and cut into slices.
4. About 15 min. before sauce is done, heat water, salt, and 1 tablespoon olive oil to boiling in a large saucepan.
5. Add noodles gradually.
6. Boil rapidly, uncovered, about 15 min., or until noodles are tender. Test tenderness by pressing a piece against side of the pan with fork or spoon. Drain noodles by turning into a colander or large sieve; rinse with hot water to remove loose starch.
7. Heat 3 tablespoons olive in a skillet.
8. Add and cook ground beef until browned, breaking into small pieces with fork or spoon.
9. Set out Mozzarella cheese and Ricotta cheese.
10. Mix together Parmesan cheese and pepper.
11. Pour ½ cup of the Tomato Meat Sauce into the baking dish. Top with a layer of noodles (about one third of the noodles) and one half of the Mozzarella cheese slices. Then add one half of the browned ground beef and one half of the hard-cooked egg slices. Sprinkle with one half of the Parmesan cheese mixture. Top with one half of the Ricotta cheese. Beginning with sauce, repeat layering, ending with Ricotta cheese. Top Ricotta cheese with ½ cup of the sauce. Arrange over this the remaining lasagne noodles. Top with more sauce.
12. Bake at 350°F about 30 min., or until mixture is bubbling. Let stand 5 to 10 min. to set layers.
13. Cut into 2-in. squares and serve topped with remaining sauce.

About 8 servings

Lobster in Ramekins

3 6-oz. cans (about 3 cups)
lobster meat
2 oz. Gruyère cheese (about
½ cup, shredded)
¼ cup butter
¼ cup sifted all-purpose
flour
1 teaspoon salt
¼ teaspoon paprika
⅛ teaspoon nutmeg
2 cups cream
2 tablespoons sherry
Parsley sprigs

1. Set out 6 shell-shaped ramekins or individual casseroles.
2. Drain and remove any bits of shell and bony tissue from contents of canned lobster meat.
3. Set aside 6 pieces of claw meat for garnish. Cut remaining meat into small pieces. Set aside.
4. Shred Gruyère cheese and set aside.
5. Heat butter in a saucepan.
6. Blend in flour, salt, paprika, and nutmeg.
7. Heat until mixture bubbles. Remove from heat and add gradually, stirring in cream.
8. Return to heat. Cook rapidly, stirring constantly, until mixture thickens. Cook 1 to 2 min. longer. Mix in the lobster meat and heat thoroughly. Remove from heat and blend in sherry.
9. Spoon mixture into ramekins. Sprinkle with the shredded cheese. Garnish each ramekin with a piece of lobster claw meat.
10. Set temperature control of range at Broil (500°F or higher). Put ramekins in broiler with tops of ramekins 2 to 3 in. from source of heat. Broil 5 min., or until cheese is bubbly.
11. Garnish with parsley sprigs.

6 servings

Turkey Lasagne

¼ **lb. bulk pork sausage**
1 **tablespoon water**
3½ **cups (28-oz. can) tomatoes, drained**
2 **tablespoons chopped parsley**
½ **teaspoon salt**
1 **teaspoon basil**
1 **teaspoon crushed rosemary**
1 **bay leaf**
1 **clove garlic, finely chopped**
1 **cup cooked turkey pieces**
1½ **cups cream-style cottage cheese**
2 **eggs, beaten**
¼ **cup finely chopped parsley**
½ **teaspoon salt**
¼ **teaspoon pepper**
4 **qts. water**
1 **tablespoon salt**
1½ **teaspoons olive oil**
½ **lb. lasagne noodles**
½ **cup (about 2 oz.) grated Parmesan cheese**
½ **lb. Swiss cheese, thinly sliced**

1. Set out an 11x7-in. shallow baking dish.
2. *For Sauce*—Break pork sausage into pieces and put into a cold skillet.
3. Add water.
4. Cover and cook 5 min. Remove cover; pour off liquid. Brown sausage meat over medium heat, moving and turning with a spoon. Drain off any excess fat from skillet.
5. Mix tomatoes, 2 tablespoons chopped parsley, ½ teaspoon salt, basil, rosemary, bay leaf, and garlic together and add to the skillet.
6. Simmer uncovered over low heat about 30 min., or until sauce is thick.
7. Meanwhile, cut into pieces enough cooked turkey to yield 1 cup cooked turkey pieces.
8. When sauce is thick, remove the bay leaf, add the turkey and cook 5 min. longer.
9. *For Cottage Cheese Mixture*—When sauce is partially done, mix cottage cheese, eggs, ¼ cup finely chopped parsley, ½ teaspoon salt, and pepper together and set aside.
10. *To Cook Noodles*—Before preparing the Cottage Cheese Mixture, heat water, 1 tablespoon salt, and olive oil to boiling in a large sauce pot.
11. Add lasagne noodles gradually.
12. Boil rapidly, uncovered, about 15 min., or until noodles are tender. Test tenderness by pressing a piece against side of the pot with fork or spoon. Drain noodles by turning into a colander or large sieve; rinse with hot water to remove loose starch.
13. *To Complete Lasagne*—Set out Parmesan cheese and Swiss cheese.
14. Spread one fourth of sauce over bottom of baking dish. Top with one third of the noodles. Spread noodles with one third of the cottage cheese mixture. Then sprinkle with one third of the Parmesan cheese and arrange one third of the Swiss cheese slices on top. Repeat the layers of sauce, noodles, cottage cheese mixture, Parmesan cheese and Swiss cheese, finishing with a layer of the sauce on top.
15. Bake at 350ºF about 30 min., or until mixture is bubbling. Let stand 5 to 10 min. to set layers before serving.

8 servings

Macaroni and Cheese

3	qts. water
1	tablespoon salt
2	cups (8 oz. pkg) uncooked macaroni (elbows or tubes broken into 2-in. pieces)
½	lb. sharp Cheddar cheese (about 2 cups, shredded)
2	cups Thin White Sauce (page 51)
½	cup buttered fine, dry bread crumbs
¼	teaspoon dry mustard

1. Grease a 1½-qt. casserole.
2. Heat water and salt to boiling in a large saucepan.
3. Add macaroni gradually.
4. Boil rapidly, uncovered, 10 to 15 min., or until tender. Test tenderness by pressing a piece against side of pan with fork or spoon. Drain macaroni by turning it into a colander or large sieve; rinse with hot water to remove loose starch. Set macaroni aside.
5. While macaroni is cooking, shred Cheddar cheese.
6. Set aside.
7. Prepare White Sauce and bread crumbs.
8. Add the cheese all at one time to the slightly cooled white sauce with dry mustard.
9. Turn one half the macaroni into casserole and pour half the cheese sauce over it. Repeat forming layers. Sprinkle crumbs over top.
10. Bake at 350°F 20 to 30 min., or until crumbs are browned.

6 servings

Savory Macaroni and Cheese: Follow recipe for Macaroni and Cheese. Reduce white sauce to 1 cup; omit dry mustard and blend into the sauce ¼ cup **chili sauce** and 2 tablespoons **Worcestershire sauce.** Proceed as in recipe.

Flavor-Filled Macaroni and Cheese: Follow recipe for Macaroni and Cheese. Decrease Cheddar cheese to 6 oz. (about 1½ cups, shredded). Omit dry mustard and blend into white sauce ⅓ cup minced **onion** and ½ teaspoon **Worcestershire sauce.** Proceed as in recipe.

Baked Cheese Fondue

¾	lb. sharp Cheddar cheese (about 3 cups, shredded)
3	cups soft bread cubes (4 to 5 slices bread)
1	tablespoon melted butter or margarine
1	teaspoon poppy seeds
2	cups milk
3	tablespoons grated onion
½	teaspoon salt
¼	teaspoon pepper
½	teaspoon dry mustard
¼	teaspoon paprika
2	drops Tabasco
4	egg yolks, well beaten
4	egg whites

1. Heat water for the hot water bath. Lightly butter a 2-qt. casserole.
2. Shred Cheddar cheese and set aside.
3. Prepare bread cubes.
4. Toss 1 cup of the bread cubes lightly with butter or margarine and poppy seeds.
5. Set cubes aside.
6. Scald milk.
7. Meanwhile, grate onion and set aside.
8. Pour scalded milk into a large mixing bowl. Add and mix in the 2 cups uncoated bread cubes, shredded cheese, onion and a mixture of salt, pepper, dry mustard, paprika, and Tabasco.
9. Mix lightly but thoroughly until cheese is melted.
10. Add egg yolks gradually, stirring constantly.
11. Beat egg whites until rounded peaks are formed.
12. Spread beaten egg whites over cheese mixture and gently fold together. Turn into the casserole. Top with poppy seed-coated bread cubes.
13. Bake in the hot water bath at 375°F 45 to 50 min., or until a silver knife inserted halfway between center and edge comes out clean.
14. Serve immediately.

About 6 servings

Cheese Soufflé

½ lb. sharp process Cheddar cheese (about 2 cups, grated)
6 tablespoons butter or margarine
6 tablespoons all-purpose flour
¾ teaspoon dry mustard
½ teaspoon salt
⅛ teaspoon white pepper
⅛ teaspoon paprika
1½ cups milk
6 egg yolks
6 egg whites

1. Set out a 2-qt. casserole; do not grease.
2. Grate Cheddar cheese and set aside.
3. Melt butter or margarine in a saucepan over low heat.
4. Blend in flour, dry mustard, salt, white pepper, and paprika.
5. Heat until mixture bubbles. Remove from heat. Add milk gradually, while stirring constantly.
6. Return to heat and bring rapidly to boiling, stirring constantly; cook 1 to 2 min. longer. Cool slightly and add the grated cheese all at one time. Stir rapidly until cheese is melted.
7. Beat egg yolks until thick and lemon-colored.
8. Slowly spoon sauce into egg yolks while stirring vigorously.
9. Beat egg whites until rounded peaks are formed and whites do not slide when bowl is partially inverted.
10. Gently spread egg-yolk mixture over beaten egg whites. Carefully fold together until just blended. Turn mixture into casserole. Insert the tip of a spoon 1 in. deep in mixture, 1 to 1½ in. from edge; run a line around mixture. (Center part of souffle will form a "hat").
11. Bake at 300°F 1 to 1¼ hrs., or until a silver knife comes out clean when inserted halfway between center and edge of soufflé.
12. Serve at once, while "top hat" is at its height.

8 to 10 servings

Cheese-Bacon Soufflé: Follow recipe for Cheese Soufflé. Dice and panbroil until crisp 5 slices **bacon.** When bacon is crisped and browned, remove from skillet; set aside on absorbent paper to drain thoroughly. Substitute 3 tablespoons of the reserved **bacon fat** for 3 tablespoons butter or margarine. Fold bacon pieces into egg whites with sauce. Proceed as in recipe.

Cheese-Mushroom Scallop

1 4-oz. can sliced mushrooms (about ½ cup, drained)
½ lb. sharp Cheddar cheese
6 slices white bread
2 tablespoons butter or margarine
Milk or cream (enough to make 1 cup liquid)
2 eggs
½ teaspoon salt
½ teaspoon paprika
⅛ teaspoon pepper

1. Grease a 1½-qt. casserole.
2. Set mushrooms aside to drain, reserving liquid.
3. Cut Cheddar cheese into ½-in. slices.
4. Trim crusts from white bread and cut into thirds.
5. Arrange some bread fingers on bottom of casserole. Cover with a layer of one-half the cheese and mushrooms. Repeat layering; top with remaining bread fingers. Dot with butter or margarine.
6. Add milk or cream to reserved mushroom liquid.
7. Beat eggs until thick and piled softly.
8. Beat salt, paprika, and pepper in the liquid.
9. Pour over layers in casserole.
10. Bake at 325°F 30 to 40 min., or until puffed and lightly browned.

About 6 servings

Puffy Cheese Omelet

4 oz. process Cheddar
cheese (about 1 cup,
grated)
2 tablespoons butter or
margarine
3 egg whites
3 tablespoons water
½ teaspoon salt
Few grains white pepper
3 egg yolks

1. Set oven temperature control at 350°F. Set out a heavy 10-in. skillet.
2. Grate Cheddar cheese and set aside.
3. Heat skillet until just hot enough to sizzle a drop of water. Heat butter or margarine in the skillet.
4. Meanwhile, beat egg whites until frothy.
5. Add water, salt, and white pepper to egg whites.
6. Continue beating until rounded peaks are formed. (The beaten egg whites should stand no longer than it takes to beat the yolks.)
7. Beat egg yolks until thick and lemon-colored.
8. Spread egg yolks over egg whites and gently fold together.
9. Turn egg mixture into skillet. Level surface gently. Cook ½ min. on top of range; lower heat and cook slowly about 10 min., or until lightly browned on bottom and puffy but still moist on top. Do not stir at any time.
10. Place skillet with omelet in the 350°F oven about 5 min. Remove and sprinkle all the grated cheese over top. Return to oven and continue baking until cheese is melted.
11. To serve, loosen edges with spatula, make a quick, shallow cut through center, and fold one side over. Gently slip omelet onto a warm serving platter. Or omit the shallow cut and folding, and using two forks, tear the omelet gently into wedges. Invert wedges on warm serving dish so browned side is on top.

3 servings

Cottage Cheese Omelet

6 eggs
6 tablespoons water or milk
¾ teaspoon salt
⅛ teaspoon pepper
1 cup cream-style cottage
cheese
2 tablespoons finely chopped pimiento
1 tablespoons minced
chives
3 tablespoons butter or
margarine

1. Set out a 10-in. skillet.
2. Beat eggs, water or milk, salt and pepper together until well blended but not foamy.
3. Mix cottage cheese, pimiento, and chives thoroughly and blend into egg mixture.
4. Heat skillet until just hot enough to sizzle a drop of water. Heat butter or margarine in skillet.
5. Pour egg mixture into skillet and reduce heat. As edges of omelet begin to thicken, draw cooked portions toward center with spoon or fork to allow uncooked mixture to flow to bottom of skillet. Shake and tilt skillet as necessary to aid flow of uncooked eggs. Do not stir.
6. When eggs no longer flow but surface is still moist, heat may be increased to brown bottom of omelet quickly. Loosen edges carefully and fold in half. Slide omelet onto a warm serving platter.

4 to 6 servings

Welsh Rabbit I

2/3 cup lukewarm beer
(measured without foam)
1 lb. sharp Cheddar cheese
(about 4 cups, shredded)
1 tablespoon butter
1/2 teaspoon Worcestershire
sauce
1/2 teaspoon dry mustard
Few grains cayenne pepper
Crisp toast slices

1. Have beer ready.
2. Shred Cheddar cheese and set aside.
3. Melt butter in top of a double boiler over simmering water.
4. Add cheese all at one time and stir occasionally until cheese begins to melt. Blend in Worcestershire sauce, dry mustard, and cayenne pepper.
5. As soon as cheese begins to melt, add very gradually, stirring constantly, 1/2 to 2/3 cup beer.
6. As soon as beer is blended in and mixture is smooth, serve immediately over crisp toast slices.

Welsh Rabbit II: Follow recipe for Welsh Rabbit. Substitute **milk** for the beer.

Welsh Rabbit III: Follow recipe for Welsh Rabbit. Substitute **process cheese food** or **sharp process Cheddar cheese** for the sharp Cheddar cheese and **milk** for the beer.

Glorified Welsh Rabbit: Follow recipe for Welsh Rabbit or either variation. Top each serving with a slice of **tomato,** two slices panbroiled **bacon** and a sprig of **parsley.**

Fluffy Cheese Potatoes

6 medium-size (about 2 lbs.)
baking potatoes
1 tablespoon fat
2 oz. process Swiss cheese
(about 1/2 cup, shredded)
4 tablespoons butter or
margarine
1/2 cup hot milk or cream (adding gradually)
3/4 teaspoon salt
1/4 teaspoon paprika
1/4 teaspoon pepper
8 slices crisp, panbroiled
bacon, crumbled
1 tablespoon finely chopped
onion
Finely chopped parsley

1. Wash and scrub potatoes with a vegetable brush.
2. Dry potatoes with absorbent paper and rub with fat.
3. Place potatoes on rack in oven.
4. Bake at 425°F 45 to 60 min., or until potatoes are soft when pressed with the fingers (protected by paper napkin).
5. While potatoes bake, shred cheese and set aside.
6. Remove potatoes from oven. To make each potato mealy, gently roll potatoes back and forth on a flat surface. Cut large potatoes into halves lengthwise or cut a thin lengthwise slice from each smaller potato. With a spoon, scoop out inside without breaking skin. Mash thoroughly or rice. Whip in, in order, butter or margarine, milk or cream (adding gradually) and a mixture of salt, paprika, and pepper until mixture is fluffy.
7. Mix in the shredded cheese and bacon and onion
8. Pile mixture lightly into potato skins, leaving tops uneven.
9. Return potatoes to oven for 8 to 10 min., or until thoroughly heated.
10. Sprinkle with parsley.

6 servings

Cheddar Cheese Potatoes: Follow recipe for Fluffy Cheese Potatoes. Substitute 1/3 cup grated **sharp Cheddar cheese** for the Swiss cheese.

Cheddar Cheese-Olive Potatoes: Follow recipe for Fluffy Cheese Potatoes. Substitute 1/3 cup grated **sharp Cheddar cheese** for the Swiss cheese. Omit the bacon and onion and add 8 to 10 **stuffed olives,** finely chopped, with the cheese. If desired, omit parsley and top potatoes with 1/3 cup crushed buttered **corn flakes** or **crumbs** before baking.

Rice-Cheese Puffs

3	cups water
1¼	teaspoons salt
½	cup rice
3	oz. sharp Cheddar cheese (about ¾ cup, grated)
4	teaspoons butter or margarine
4	teaspoons all-purpose flour
¼	teaspoon salt
	Few grains pepper
⅓	cup milk
½	teaspoon grated onion
¼	teaspoon dry mustard
¼	teaspoon Worcestershire sauce
5	drops Tabasco
1	egg, slightly beaten
1	tablespoon milk
½	cup fine, dry bread crumbs (about 1½ slices bread)

A deep saucepan or automatic deep fryer will be needed.

1. *To Cook Rice* — Bring water and salt to boiling in a large saucepan.
2. Add rice gradually to water so boiling will not stop. (The Rice Industry no longer considers it necessary to wash rice before cooking.) Boil rice rapidly, uncovered, 15 to 20 min., or until a kernel is soft when pressed between fingers.
3. Drain in a colander or sieve and rinse with hot water to remove loose starch. (Cooked rice prepared from packaged-precooked rice may be used if directions on package are followed carefully for amounts and timing.)
4. *To Prepare Cheese Mixture* — Set out a medium-size saucepan.
5. Grate cheese and set aside.
6. Melt butter or margarine in the saucepan over low heat.
7. Blend in flour, salt, and pepper.
8. Heat until mixture bubbles. Remove from heat. Add milk gradually while stirring constantly.
9. Return to heat and bring rapidly to boiling, stirring constantly; cook 1 to 2 min. longer.
10. Cool sauce slightly and add the grated cheese all at one time. Stir sauce rapidly until cheese is melted. Stir in onion, dry mustard, Worcestershire sauce, and Tabasco.
11. Mix with cooked rice and place in refrigerator to chill (about 1 hr.).
12. About 20 min. before deep frying, fill the sauce pan or deep fryer with fat and heat to 375°F.
13. *To Complete Puffs* — Shape chilled mixture into 2-in. balls, using about 1 tablespoon of the mixture for each ball. Dip into a mixture of egg and milk.
14. Coat balls by rolling in dry bread crumbs.
15. Deep fry cheese balls in heated fat. Fry only as many balls at one time as will float uncrowded one layer deep in fat. Turn balls with a fork as they rise to surface and several times during cooking (do not pierce). Fry 1 to 2 min., or until balls are golden brown. Lift them out with a slotted spoon and drain over fat for a few seconds before removing to absorbent paper.
16. Serve hot with your favorite tomato sauce and buttered green beans.

About 12 puffs

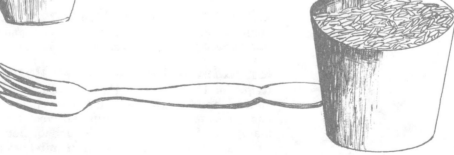

Cheese-Tomato Supper Dish

6	eggs
¾	lb. sharp Cheddar cheese (about 3 cups, grated)
⅔	cup butter or margarine
¼	cup minced onion
1	cup mushrooms, cleaned and sliced
2	tablespoons all-purpose flour
½	teaspoon dry mustard
¼	teaspoon salt
	Few grains cayenne pepper
½	cup milk
½	teaspoon Worcestershire sauce
1	10½- to 11-oz. can (about 1¼ cups) condensed tomato soup

1. Hard cook eggs.
2. Peel, cut into quarters lengthwise and set aside.
3. Meanwhile, grate Cheddar cheese and set aside.
4. Heat butter or margarine in a chafing pan or in top of double boiler over direct heat.
5. Add onion and mushrooms and cook over medium heat, occasionally moving and turning with a spoon, until mushrooms are tender.
6. With slotted spoon, remove mushrooms to a small bowl. Set aside.
7. Blend in a mixture of flour, dry mustard, salt, and cayenne pepper.
8. Heat until mixture bubbles. Remove from heat. Add milk and Worchestershire sauce gradually, and contents of condensed tomato soup.
9. Place chafing pan on top of double boiler over simmering water. Add the grated cheese all at one time. Stir constantly until cheese is melted. Blend in the hard-cooked egg quarters and the vegetables. Garnish with minced parsley.
10. Serve with toast fingers or bread sticks.

About 8 servings

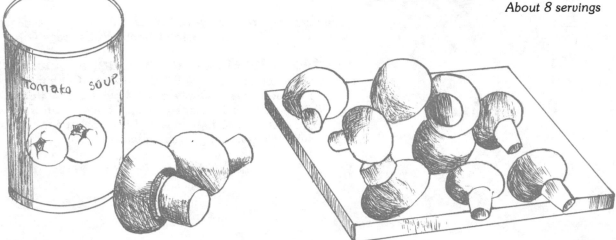

Asparagus with Cheese Sauce

3	lbs. asparagus
2	cups Cheese Sauce (page 51)
6	slices bread
	Butter or margarine
	Few grains paprika

1. Break off and discard lower parts of stalks of asparagus, as far down as they will snap.
2. Wash remaining portions of stalks thoroughly. If necessary, remove scales to dislodge any sand. Cook 10 to 20 min., or until asparagus is tender. (Or cook contents of three 10-oz. pkgs. frozen asparagus.)
3. Meanwhile, prepare Cheese Sauce. Keep sauce warm by setting it over hot water. Cover tightly.
4. Toast bread.
5. Spread one side of each slice with butter or margarine.
6. When asparagus is tender, drain if necessary. Arrange servings of asparagus on slices of toast. Spoon hot sauce over asparagus. Sprinkle each serving with paprika.
7. Serve immediately.

6 servings

Cheese-Rice Filled Tomatoes

⅓ **cup packaged, precooked rice (about 1 cup, cooked)**
½ **lb. process Swiss cheese (about 2 cups, shredded)**
6 **large, firm tomatoes**
2 **tablespoons butter**
½ **cup chopped onion**
¼ **cup chopped celery**
½ **cup (1 4-oz. can drained) canned sliced mushrooms**
1 **teaspoon salt**
¼ **marjoram**
⅛ **teaspoon pepper**
Water cress

1. Thoroughly grease a shallow 2-qt. baking dish.
2. Set out a skillet.
3. Cook rice according to directions on package.
4. Meanwhile, shred Swiss cheese and set aside.
5. Rinse, cut out and discard stem end from tomatoes.
6. Cut a slice about ¼ in. thick from top of each tomato; reserve. With a spoon, scoop out pulp from tomatoes. Drain excess liquid from pulp; reserve pulp. Set tomatoes aside to drain.
7. Heat butter in the skillet.
8. Add onion and celery to skillet and cook over medium heat until onion is transparent.
9. Mix together the rice, contents of skillet, shredded cheese, tomato pulp and sliced mushrooms, salt, marjoram, and pepper.
10. Spoon mixture into tomato shells. Replace tops. Place in baking dish.
11. Bake at 350°F 15 min., or until thoroughly heated.
12. Garnish centers of tomato tops with water cress.
13. Serve immediately.

6 servings

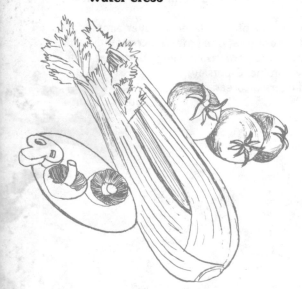

*One-third cup **rice** may be substituted for the packaged precooked rice. Cook as in **Rice-Cheese Puffs** (page 46).

Stuffed Tomatoes with Cheese Sauce:
Follow recipe for Cheese-Rice Filled Tomatoes. Cut a thin slice from top of each tomato. Omit shredded Swiss cheese from filling. While tomatoes bake prepare 1 cup **Cheese Sauce** (page 47). Serve each tomato topped with 2 or 3 tablespoons of the sauce. Substitute **parsley** garnish for water cress.

Blue Cheese Eggplant en Casserole

1 **large eggplant (about 1½ lbs.)**
⅔ **cup (about 1 large) chopped onion**
1 **cup fine, dry bread crumbs (about 3 slices bread)**
½ **cup (about 2 oz.) crumbled Blue cheese**
1 **egg, well beaten**
⅛ **teaspoon marjoram**
3 **tablespoons butter**

1. Grease a 2-qt. casserole.
2. Rinse, pare and dice eggplant.
3. Combine in a saucepan with chopped onion.
4. Cook 7 to 10 min., or until eggplant is just tender when pierced with a fork. Drain immediately.
5. Meanwhile, set out bread crumbs.
6. Toss together the vegetables, ¾ cup of the bread crumbs and Blue cheese, egg, and marjoram.
7. Turn into casserole. Top with the remaining bread crumbs and dot with butter.
8. Bake at 350° 30 to 35 min.

8 servings

Cauliflower Casserole

1	large head cauliflower
4	oz. sharp Cheddar cheese (about 1 cup, shredded)
3	tablespoons butter
¾	cup small bread cubes
¼	cup butter
¼	cup minced onion
3	tablespoons all-purpose flour
½	teaspoon salt
	Few grains pepper
1⅔	cups undiluted evaporated milk
⅔	cup water
2	egg yolks, slightly beaten
½	cup grated Parmesan cheese
1	tablespoon lemon juice

1. Butter a 1½-qt. casserole.
2. Remove leaves, cut off all the woody base and trim off any blemishes from cauliflower.
3. Wash cauliflower thoroughly and carefully separate into flowerets. Cook in boiling, salted water 8 to 10 min., or until tender but still firm.
4. Meanwhile, shred Cheddar cheese and set aside.
5. Heat butter in a skillet.
6. Add bread cubes to skillet, tossing to coat evenly.
7. When bread cubes are lightly browned, remove from heat and set aside.
8. When cauliflower is cooked, turn into colander and set aside to drain thoroughly.
9. *For Sauce*—Melt butter in top of a double boiler over direct heat.
10. Add onion and cook until onion is transparent.
11. Blend in flour, salt, and pepper.
12. Heat until mixture bubbles. Remove from heat. Add gradually, stirring in evaporated milk and water.
13. Return to heat and cook rapidly, stirring constantly, until sauce thickens. Cook 1 to 2 min., longer. Vigorously stir about 3 tablespoons of sauce into egg yolks.
14. Immediately return mixture to double boiler.
15. Cook over simmering water 3 to 5 min. Stir slowly to keep mixture cooking evenly. Remove from simmering water and cool sauce slightly.
16. Add Parmesan cheese all at one time and blend.
17. Blend in lemon juice.
18. Arrange one half of cauliflowerets in casserole. Cover with one half of sauce. Top with remaining cauliflowerets and sauce. Sprinkle the shredded cheese over top. Arrange bread cubes in a border around top of casserole.
19. Bake at 350°F about 30 min., or until lightly browned and thoroughly heated.

About 6 servings

Parmesan Cheese Sauce

2	tablespoons butter
1	tablespoon all-purpose flour
1	cup thick sour cream
1	egg yolk, slightly beaten
¼	cup (about 1 oz.) grated Parmesan cheese

1. Melt butter in top of a double boiler over low heat.
2. Blend in flour.
3. Heat until mixture bubbles. Remove from heat and add sour cream very gradually.
4. Cook over simmering water, stirring constantly, 1 to 2 min. longer. Remove from heat and vigorously stir about 3 tablespoons of the hot sauce into egg yolk.
5. Immediately return mixture to double boiler. Cook over simmering water 3 to 5 min. Stir slowly to keep mixture cooking evenly. Remove from heat and add (all at one time) Parmesan cheese.
6. Blend thoroughly.

About ¾ cup sauce

Eggplant Casserole

1	cup fine, dry bread crumbs (about 3 slices bread)
2	medium-size eggplants (about 1 lb. each)
1	egg, slightly beaten
¼	cup milk
½	teaspoon salt
½	cup butter
6	oz. sharp Cheddar cheese (about 1½ cups, shredded)
3	tablespoons butter
¼	cup finely chopped onion
2	tablespoons minced green pepper
1	6-oz. can tomato paste
1½	cups water
1	teaspoon salt
¼	teaspoon pepper

1. Set out a large, heavy skillet; butter a 2-qt. casserole having a tight-fitting cover.
2. *For Eggplant Slices*—Set out bread crumbs.
3. Wash eggplants, pare and cut crosswise into ½-in. slices.
4. Mix egg, milk and salt together in a shallow bowl.
5. Dip eggplant slices into egg mixture. Then coat with bread crumbs, coating evenly on both sides.
6. Set out butter.
7. Heat ¼ cup of the butter in the skillet over low heat. Add as many eggplant slices at one time as will lie flat in skillet. Cook over medium heat until lightly browned; turn and brown other side. Add the extra butter as necessary. Set slices aside and keep them warm.
8. While eggplant slices are browning, shred Cheddar cheese and set aside.
9. *For Tomato Sauce*—Heat butter in the skillet.
10. Add and cook onion and green pepper over medium heat until onion is tender.
11. Blend in tomato paste.
12. Remove from heat.
13. *For Casserole*—Arrange a layer of eggplant slices in bottom of casserole. Pour some of sauce over slices and sprinkle with part of cheese. Repeat layering, ending with cheese.
14. Cover casserole and bake at 325°F 20 min. Remove cover and bake about 5 min. longer, or until eggplant is golden brown and cheese is bubbly.

6 to 8 servings.

Tomato Meat Sauce

¼	cup olive oil
½	cup (about 1 medium-size) chopped onion
½	lb. beef chuck
½	lb. pork shoulder
7	cups (2 28-oz. cans) tomatoes, sieved
1	tablespoon salt
1	bay leaf
¾	cup (1 6-oz. can) tomato paste
½	cup water

1. Set out a large sauce pot having a tight-fitting cover.
2. Heat olive oil in the sauce pot.
3. Add onion and cook about 3 min.
4. Add beef chuck and pork shoulder to the sauce pot and cook, turning to brown on all sides.
5. Add slowly a mixture of tomatoes, salt, and bay leaf.
6. Cover sauce pot and simmer over very low heat, about 2½ hrs.
7. Add tomato paste.
8. Simmer uncovered over very low heat, stirring occasionally, about 2 hrs., or until sauce is thickened.
9. If sauce becomes too thick, add water.
10. Remove meat and bay leaf from sauce. Serve sauce over cooked spaghetti accompanied by quantities of grated Parmesan cheese, or use in other recipes where a tomato sauce would be desirable.

About 4 cups sauce

Cheese Sauce

1C. **1** oz. Cheddar cheese or process cheese food (about ¼ cup, grated)

8tbl. **2** tablespoons butter or margarine

8tbl. **2** tablespoons all-purpose flour

1tsp. **¼** teaspoon salt

¼ teaspoon dry mustard

Few grains cayenne pepper

Few grains pepper

4C. **1** cup milk

1. Grate Cheddar cheese or process cheese and set aside.
2. Melt butter or margarine in a saucepan over low heat.
3. Blend in flour, salt, dry mustard, cayenne pepper, and pepper.
4. Heat until mixture bubbles. Remove from heat.
5. Add milk gradually, stirring in.
6. Cook rapidly, stirring constantly, until sauce thickens. Cook 1 to 2 min. longer. Remove from heat. Cool sauce slightly.
7. Add grated cheese all at one time, stirring until cheese is melted.

About 1 cup sauce

4 cups

Medium White Sauce: Follow recipe for Cheese Sauce. Omit grated cheese, dry mustard and cayenne pepper.

Thick White Sauce: Follow recipe for Medium White Sauce. Use 3 to 4 tablespoons flour and 3 to 4 tablespoons butter or margarine. Use in preparation of souffles and croquettes.

Thin White Sauce: Follow recipe for Medium White Sauce. Use 1 tablespoon flour and 1 tablespoon butter or margarine.

Mornay Sauce

¾ cup Quick Chicken Broth (page 11)

3 tablespoons butter or margarine

3 tablespoons all-purpose flour

¾ cup cream

2 egg yolks, slightly beaten

⅓ cup grated Parmesan or finely-cut Gruyère cheese

1 tablespoon butter

1. Prepare Quick Chicken Broth.
2. Set aside.
3. Heat butter or margarine in top of double boiler over low heat.
4. Blend in flour.
5. Heat until mixture bubbles. Remove from heat and add the chicken broth and cream gradually, stirring in.
6. Return to heat and bring rapidly to boiling stirring constantly; cook 1 to 2 min. longer. Remove from heat and vigorously stir about 3 tablespoons of sauce into egg yolks.
7. Immediately return mixture to double boiler. Cook over simmering water 3 to 5 min. Stir slowly to keep mixture cooking evenly. Cool slightly. Add Parmesan or finely-cut Gruyère cheese and butter all at one time and blend in until cheese is melted.
8. Serve hot.

About 2 cups sauce

Salads

Nippy Cheese Freeze Salad

10   **stuffed olives**
3   **oz. natural cheese food**
½   **cup thick sour cream**
1   **teaspoon lemon juice**
3   **drops Tabasco**
     Lettuce
     Curly endive
     Romaine
     Water cress
1   **clove garlic, cut in halves**

1. *For Nippy Cheese Freeze*—Set refrigerator control at colder operating temperature.
2. Chop olives and set aside.
3. Put cheese food into a small bowl and mash with a fork.
4. Add sour cream gradually, blending until mixture is smooth.
5. Blend in the chopped olives and lemon juice and Tabasco.
6. Turn mixture into refrigerator tray. Put into freezing compartment of refrigerator and freeze until mixture is firm.
7. *For Tossed Salad*—Wash and discard bruised leaves from lettuce, curly endive, romaine, and water cress, drain thoroughly and pat dry (using as much of each green as desired).
8. Tear greens into bite-size pieces (enough to yield about 2 qts. greens). Put into a plastic bag and chill in refrigerator at least 1 hr.
9. When ready to serve, rub a salad bowl with cut surface of garlic clove.
10. Cut the frozen cheese mixture into small cubes. Put the chilled greens into the salad bowl and toss lightly with French dressing. Add the cheese cubes and toss just enough to distribute the cubes evenly throughout the greens.
11. Serve immediately.

6 to 8 servings

Royal Swiss Cheese Salad Bowl

½ lb. natural Swiss cheese
French dressing
Bibb lettuce
Leaf lettuce
Water cress

1. Cut Swiss cheese into thin strips.
2. Put cheese into a shallow bowl and cover with French dressing.
3. Marinate in refrigerator 1 hr.
4. Wash, discard bruised leaves from bibb lettuce, leaf lettuce, and water cress, drain thoroughly and pat dry (using as much of each green as desired).
5. Arrange bibb and leaf lettuce in a large salad bowl. Fill center with water cress. Put salad bowl into plastic bag or cover with aluminum foil. Chill in refrigerator at least 1 hr.
6. Drain marinated cheese strips. Arrange in salad bowl on both sides of water cress. Serve with additional French dressing.

Cheese Mousse

¾ cup heavy cream
7 oz. cream cheese
1 package unflavored gelatin
½ teaspoon salt
½ teaspoon paprika powder
1 tablespoon chopped chives

Garnish:
Watercress
2 sliced cucumbers
6 radishes

1. Whip the heavy cream till stiff. Stir the cream cheese until smooth and add half the cream to it.
2. Place the gelatin in 2 tablespoons water and dissolve over low heat. Stir the gelatin in the cream and cream cheese mixture and add the rest of the whipped cream. Add seasonings.
3. Pour the cheese cream into a water-rinsed ring mold. Place in refrigerator to set. Serve garnished with **watercress, cucumbers** and **radishes.**

Serves 4

Pear and Frozen Cheese Salad

4 oz. Roquefort or Blue cheese (1 cup, crumbled)
½ cup chopped celery
3 oz. (1 pkg.) cream cheese
¼ cup mayonnaise
1 tablespoon lemon juice
¼ teaspoon salt
⅛ teaspoon pepper
½ cup chilled whipping cream
4 chilled, ripe Bartlett pears
Lemon juice
Curly endive, water cress, or other salad greens
French dressing

1. Crumble Roquefort or Blue cheese and set aside.
2. Prepare celery and set aside.
3. Beat cream cheese until fluffy.
4. Mix in mayonnaise and lemon juice, and a mixture of salt and pepper, stirring until thoroughly blended after each addition.
5. Stir in the crumbled cheese and chopped celery. Set mixture aside.
6. Using the chilled bowl and beater, beat whipping cream until cream is of medium consistency (piles softly).
7. Gently fold into cheese mixture. Turn into the chilled refrigerator tray. Put into freezing compartment of refrigerator and freeze until cheese mixture is firm.
8. When ready to serve, cut frozen cheese into 1-in. cubes.
9. *For Bartlett Pear Salad* — Rinse well, cut into halves and core Bartlett pears.
10. Brush cut sides of pears with lemon juice.
11. Place salad greens on each of 8 chilled salad plates.
12. Put one pear half, cut side up, on each plate. Place two or three Frozen Roquefort or Blue Cheese Cubes in hollow of each pear half. Or arrange greens, pear halves and cheese cubes on a large chilled serving plate.
13. Serve immediately with French dressing.

8 servings

Special Salad Bowl

1	large head lettuce
1	head curly endive
3	finely chopped green onions (peeled, rinsed, green tops cut off to within 3 in. of white part)
4	eggs
1	cup cooked chicken or turkey, cut into thin strips
2	tablespoons tarragon vinegar
4	oz. Roquefort cheese (about 1 cup, crumbled)
¾	cup mayonnaise
3	tablespoons chili sauce
3	tablespoons sweet pickle relish
½	teaspoon celery salt

1. A large salad bowl will be needed.
2. Rinse, remove core, discard bruised leaves from lettuce and curly endive and pat dry.
3. Finely cut endive with scissors. Tear lettuce into bite-size pieces. Toss greens with green onions.
4. Put into a large plastic bag and chill in refrigerator at least 1 hr.
5. Meanwhile, hard-cook eggs and set aside.
6. Mix together chicken or turkey, and tarragon vinegar in a bowl.
7. Set aside.
8. Crumble Roquefort cheese and set aside.
9. Gently mix mayonnaise, chili sauce, relish, and salt together.
10. Mix together in the salad bowl the greens, chicken or turkey mixture and the cheese. Pour the dressing over the mixture and toss lightly. Cut the hard-cooked eggs into quarters and arrange on salad.
11. Serve immediately.

8 servings

Molded Pineapple-Cheese Salad

1	20-oz. can chilled, crushed pineapple (about 1¾ cups pineapple, drained)
2	env. unflavored gelatin Water
½	cup sugar
½	teaspoon salt
1	cup unsweetened pineapple juice
1	cup orange juice
3	drops yellow food coloring
1	lb. cream cheese, softened
3	tablespoons lemon juice
2	teaspoons grated lemon peel
	Honeydew melon balls
	Frosted grapes
	Mint leaves

1. Set out a 2-qt. ring mold.
2. Drain pineapple, reserving syrup. Set aside.
3. Pour into a small bowl ½ cup of the reserved pineapple syrup. Sprinkle evenly over syrup unflavored gelatin.
4. Let gelatin stand until softened.
5. Add water to remaining reserved pineapple syrup, if necessary, to make 1 cup liquid.
6. Heat until very hot. Remove from heat and immediately add softened gelatin, stirring until gelatin is completely dissolved. Add, stirring until dissolved sugar and salt.
7. Stir in pineapple juice, orange juice and yellow food coloring.
8. Chill until mixture is slightly thicker than consistency of thick, unbeaten egg white.
9. Lightly oil the mold with salad oil or cooking oil (not olive oil); set aside to drain.
10. Put cream cheese into a bowl.
11. Add lemon juice and lemon peel gradually, beating in.
12. When gelatin mixture is of the same consistency as the cheese mixture, stir several tablespoons of the gelatin mixture into cheese mixture. Continue to add gelatin mixture slowly, beating constantly, until well blended. Blend in crushed pineapple. Turn mixture into prepared mold. Place mold in refrigerator to chill until firm.
13. Unmold onto chilling serving plate.
14. If desired, fill center of salad ring with honeydew melon balls.
15. Garnish with frosted grapes and mint leaves.
16. *For Frosted Grapes*—Beat 1 egg white until frothy. Dip grapes in beaten egg white. Shake off excess, then dip grapes in sugar. Set aside to dry. Chill in refrigerator if desired.

Frozen Fruit Salad

¼ **cup sugar**
1½ **teaspoons cornstarch**
 Few grains salt
¼ **cup unsweetened pineap-**
 ple juice
1 **egg yolk, slightly beaten**
1 **egg white**
1 **tablespoon sugar**
½ **cup lukewarm unsweetened**
 pineapple juice
1 **tablespoon butter**
⅓ **cup chilled whipping**
 cream
½ **cup (about 3 oz.) almonds**
1 **15¼-oz. can crushed**
 pineapple (about 1½ cups,
 drained)
½ **cup maraschino cherries**
½ **cup (about 3 oz.) pitted**
 dates
24 **(6 oz.) marshmallows**
8 **oz. cream cheese, softened**
¼ **cup mayonnaise**
1 **cup chilled whipping**
 cream

1. *For Pineapple Dressing*—(About 2 cups dressing) Sift together into top of double boiler sugar, cornstarch, and salt.
2. Stir in ¼ cup unsweetened pineapple juice.
3. Stirring gently and constantly, bring rapidly to boiling over direct heat. Cook 3 min. Place over simmering water. Vigorously stir about 3 tablespoons of the hot mixture into egg yolk.
4. Immediately blend into mixture in double boiler, stirring constantly. Cook over simmering water 3 to 5 min. Stir slowly to keep mixture cooking evenly. Remove double boiler top from simmering water.
5. Beat egg white until frothy.
6. Add sugar gradually, continuing to beat.
7. Beat until rounded peaks are formed. Gently blend egg white into pineapple mixture. Add ½ cup lukewarm unsweetened pineapple apple juice gradually, stirring constantly.
8. Return double boiler top to simmering water and continue to cook until thick and smooth, stirring constantly (about 10 min.). Add and stir butter into mixture.
9. Remove from heat and set aside to cool. Chill in refrigerator.
10. Before serving, using a chilled bowl and beater, beat whipping cream until of medium consistency (piles softly).
11. Carefully blend whipped cream into pineapple dressing.
12. *For Salad*—Set refrigerator control for colder operating temperature. Put a bowl and rotary beater in refrigerator to chill. Set out a 1½-qt. mold or large refrigerator tray.
13. Blanch, toast and salt almonds.
14. Chop coarsely and set aside.
15. Set out crushed pineapple to drain, reserving syrup.
16. Cut maraschino cherries into quarters and set aside to drain. (To avoid pink-tinted mixture, drain cherries thoroughly.)
17. Cut dates into slivers and set aside.
18. Cut marshmallows into eighths and set aside.
19. Beat until well blended 3 tablespoons of the reserved pineapple syrup and cream cheese.
20. Mix in mayonnaise.
21. Gently mix in nuts, fruits and marshmallows.
22. Using the chilled bowl and beater, beat whipping cream until cream is of medium consistency (piles softly).
23. Lightly spread over cheese mixture and fold together. Turn into mold or refrigerator tray. Freeze (2 to 4 hrs.).
24. Unmold onto chilled serving plate and garnish base with fruit and sprigs of mint or water cress. Or serve slices or wedges of the salad on chilled individual salad plates.
25. Serve with pineapple dressing.

8 to 10 servings

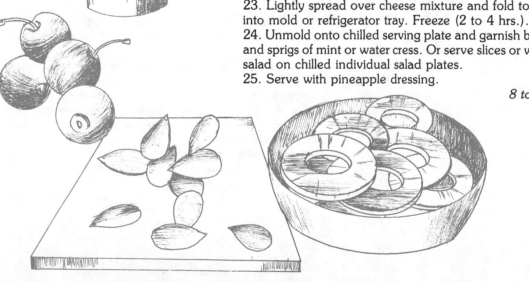

Colorful Layered Salad

1	**3-oz. pkg. lime-flavored gelatin**
1	**cup very hot water**
1	**cup cold water**
½	**cup halved seeded or seedless green grapes**
1	**cup mayonnaise**
1	**3-oz. pkg. lemon-flavored gelatin**
1	**cup very hot water**
1	**cup unsweetened pineapple juice**
1	**tablespoon sugar**
¼	**teaspoon salt**
3	**oz. (1 pkg.) cream cheese, softened**
1	**3-oz. pkg. raspberry-flavored gelatin**
1	**cup very hot water**
1	**cup cold water**
1	**teaspoon lemon juice**
1	**banana with all-yellow or brown-flecked peel**
	Lettuce leaves
	Red and green maraschino cherries, drained

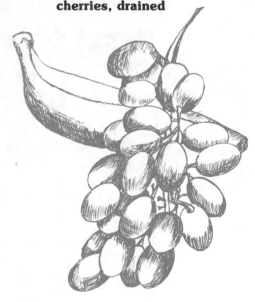

1. Lightly oil a 9½x5¼x2¾-in. loaf pan with salad or cooking oil (not olive oil); set aside to drain.
2. *For Green Layer*—Empty lime-flavored gelatin into a bowl.
3. Add 1 cup very hot water and stir until the gelatin is completely dissolved.
4. Stir 1 cup cold water into gelatin mixture.
5. Pour into the loaf pan a small amount of the gelatin mixture (enough to make a thin layer). Chill in refrigerator until slightly set.
6. Chill remaining gelatin mixture until slightly thicker than consistency of thick, unbeaten egg white. When gelatin mixture in mold is of the deisred consistency, arrange grapes in rows in the slightly set gelatin, cut sides up.
7. Carefully spoon remaining gelatin over grapes. Chill in refrigerator until slightly set.
8. Meanwhile, prepare Cream Cheese Layer.
9. *For Cream Cheese Layer*—Put mayonnaise into a bowl and set aside.
10. Empty lemon-flavored gelatin into another bowl.
11. Add 1 cup very hot water and stir until gelatin is completely dissolved.
12. Stir pineapple juice, sugar, and salt into gelatin mixture.
13. Add gelatin mixture gradually to mayonnaise, stirring constantly. Chill until mixture begins to gel (get slightly thicker).
14. Meanwhile, beat cream cheese until of medium consistency.
15. When gelatin mixture is of about the same consistency as the cheese, stir several tablespoons of the gelatin mixture into the cheese. Continue to add gelatin mixture slowly, beating constantly until well blended.
16. When green layer in mold is of the proper consistency, immediately spoon cheese mixture over it, spreading evenly to corners. (Layers should be almost same consistency when combined to avoid separation of layers when unmolded.) Chill in refrigerator until slightly set.
17. Meanwhile, prepare Red Layer.
18. *For Red Layer*—Empty raspberry-flavored gelatin into a bowl.
19. Add and stir 1 cup very hot water until the gelatin is completely dissolved.
20. Stir 1 cup cold water and lemon juice into gelatin mixture.
21. Chill until slightly thicker than consistency of thick, unbeaten egg white.
22. Meanwhile, peel and slice banana crosswise into ¼-in. thick slices.
23. When gelatin mixture is of desired consistency, fold in banana slices. When cream cheese layer in mold is about the same consistency, turn banana mixture over the cheese layer. Chill in refrigerator until firm.
24. Unmold onto chilled serving plate.
25. Garnish with lettuce leaves and maraschino cherries.
26. Cut into ¾-in. slices and serve.

About 12 servings

Jellied Peach and Cheese Salad

1	3-oz. pkg. lemon-flavored gelatin
1	cup very hot water
1	cup cold water
4	medium-size (about 1 lb.) firm, ripe peaches
1	teaspoon lemon juice
½	cup cold water
1	env. unflavored gelatin
1	cup cream-style cottage cheese
3	oz. (1 pkg.) cream cheese, softened
½	cup milk
½	cup mayonnaise
1	tablespoon lemon juice
¼	teaspoon salt
	Pineapple slices, cut in halves
	Fresh, ripe whole strawberries or Bing cherries
	Curly endive

1. *For First Layer*—Lightly oil a 2-qt. oval mold with salad or cooking oil (not olive oil); set aside to drain.
2. Empty lemon-flavored gelatin into a bowl.
3. Add 1 cup very hot water and stir until gelatin is completely dissolved.
4. Stir 1 cup cold water into gelatin mixture.
5. Pour a small amount of gelatin mixture (enough to make a thin layer) into bottom of mold. Chill in refrigerator until slightly set.
6. Chill remaining gelatin mixture until slightly thicker than consistency of thick, unbeaten egg white.
7. Meanwhile, rinse, peel, cut into halves and pit peaches.
8. Quickly blot peaches on absorbent paper, if necessary. Cut peaches into slices. Add lemon juice to peaches and mix lightly.
9. Set aside.
10. When gelatin in mold is slightly set, immediately remove from refrigerator. Arrange peach slices in two lengthwise rows in the gelatin layer in mold. Carefully spoon in remaining gelatin mixture. Chill in refrigerator until slightly set.
11. *For Second Layer*—Meanwhile pour ½ cup cold water into a small bowl.
12. Sprinkle unflavored gelatin evenly over cold water.
13. Let the gelatin stand until softened. Dissolve completely by placing bowl over a pan of very hot water.
14. Put cottage, cream cheese, milk, mayonnaise, lemon juice, and salt into a bowl and beat until well blended and creamy.
15. When gelatin is dissolved, stir it and blend into cheese mixture. When first layer in mold is slightly set, immediately turn cheese mixture onto it and gently spread out in an even layer. (The two layers should be of about the same consistency when combined to avoid separation of layers when unmolded.) Chill in refrigerator until firm.
16. Unmold onto a chilled platter. Garnish with pineapple slices.

6 to 8 servings

Blue Cheese Dressing

4	oz. (about 1 cup) Blue cheese
2	tablespoons wine vinegar
1	tablespoon lemon juice
½	teaspoon Worcestershire sauce
½	teaspoon sugar
½	teaspoon dry mustard
½	teaspoon paprika
¼	teaspoon salt
⅛	teaspoon pepper
⅔	cup salad oil

1. Crumble Blue cheese into a bowl.
2. Blend in wine vinegar, lemon juice, and Worcestershire sauce until smooth.
3. Add and stir until blended a mixture of sugar, dry mustard, paprika, salt and pepper.
4. Add salad oil gradually, beating constantly.
5. Store in covered container in refrigerator. Mix well before using.

About 1¼ cups dressing

Molded Cottage Cheese and Olive Salad

¾   **cup cold water**
2   **env. unflavored gelatin**
1¼   **cups (10½- to 11-oz. can) condensed tomato soup**
1   **cup chopped ripe olives**
½   **cup (about 1 stalk) chopped celery**
⅓   **cup chopped green pepper**
2   **tablespoons chopped pimiento**
1   **tablespoon minced onion**
2   **cups cream-style cottage cheese**
⅓   **cup mayonnaise**
2   **tablespoons lemon juice**
2   **teaspoons Worcestershire sauce**
  Few grains pepper
  Whole ripe olives
  Bits of pimiento
  Green pepper strips

1. Set out an 8½x4½x2½-in. loaf pan.
2. Pour ¾ cup cold water into a small bowl.
3. Sprinkle unflavored gelatin over water.
4. Let gelatin stand until softened.
5. Meanwhile, heat tomato soup until very hot.
6. Remove from heat, add softened gelatin and stir until gelatin is completely dissolved. Chill until gelatin mixture begins to gel (gets slightly thicker).
7. Meanwhile, prepare olives, celery, green pepper, chopped pimiento, and onion and set aside.
8. Lightly oil loaf pan with salad or cooking oil (not olive oil); set aside to drain.
9. Force cottage cheese through sieve into a bowl.
10. Blend with cheese, mayonnaise, lemon juice, Worcestershire sauce, and pepper.
11. Blend in vegetables and add to gelatin mixture. Turn into prepared loaf pan. Chill in refrigerator until firm.
12. Unmold onto chilled serving plate. Garnish with olives, pimiento, and pepper strips.
13. Arrange small **lettuce leaves** and additional **whole ripe olives** around salad loaf.

About 8 servings

Roquefort-Cream Dressing

2   **oz. (about ½ cup) Roquefort or Blue cheese**
2   **tablespoons water**
1   **cup thick sour cream**
3   **tablespoons chopped chives**
½   **teaspoon salt**

1. Crumble Roquefort or Blue cheese into a bowl.
2. Mix into water to form a smooth paste.
3. Blend in sour cream, chopped chives and salt.
4. Store in covered container in refrigerator.

About 1½ cups dressing

Roquefort-Mayonnaise Dressing: Follow recipe for Roquefort-Cream Dressing. Substitute ¾ cup **mayonnaise** and ⅓ cup **cream** for sour cream.

Roquefort French Dressing

¾   **cup olive oil**
¼   **cup tarragon or cider vinegar**
¼   **teaspoon Worcestershire sauce**
1   **clove garlic, cut into halves**
1   **teaspoon sugar**
½   **teaspoon salt**
¼   **teaspoon paprika**
¼   **teaspoon dry mustard**
⅛   **teaspoon pepper**
⅛   **teaspoon thyme**
3   **oz. (about ¾ cup) Roquefort cheese, crumbled**
2   **teaspoons water**

1. Combine olive oil, tarragon or cider vinegar, Worcestershire sauce, garlic, sugar, salt, paprika, dry mustard, pepper, and thyme in a screw-top jar.
2. Shake well. Chill in refrigerator.
3. Just before serving, blend Roquefort cheese and water until smooth.
4. Remove garlic. Beat or shake dressing thoroughly; add slowly to cheese, blending after each addition.

About 1 cup dressing

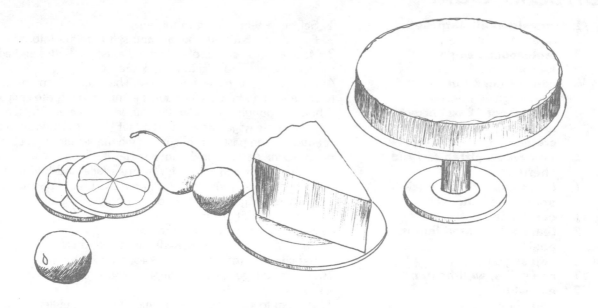

Desserts

Luscious Lemon Cheese Cake

24	slices (6 oz.) zwieback (or enough to yield 2⅔ cups crumbs)
½	cup sifted confectioners' sugar
3	teaspoons grated lemon peel
½	cup butter or margarine, softened
2½	lbs. cream cheese, softened
½	teaspoon vanilla extract
1¾	cups sugar
3	tablespoons all-purpose flour
5	eggs
2	egg yolks
¼	cup heavy cream

1. Butter bottom and sides of a 9-inch spring-form pan.
2. *For Crust*—Prepare crumbs from zwieback.
3. Turn crumbs into a bowl. Stir in confectioners' sugar and lemon peel.
4. Using a fork or pastry blender, blend in butter or margarine.
5. Reserve ¾ cup of mixture for topping; turn remainder into the spring-form pan. With fingers or back of spoon, press crumbs very firmly into an even layer on bottom of pan and up around sides to the rim; set aside.
6. *For Filling*—Put into a bowl and blend together cream cheese, lemon peel and vanilla extract.
7. Add sugar and flour gradually, blending until smooth after each addition.
8. Beat together and add gradually to cream cheese mixture, 5 eggs, and 2 egg yolks, beating thoroughly after each addition.
9. Blend in heavy cream.
10. Turn into the pan. Spread evenly. Sprinkle reserved crumb mixture evenly over top.
11. Bake at 250°F 1 hr. Turn off heat. Let stand in oven 1 hr. longer. Remove to cooling rack to cool completely (4 to 6 hrs.).
12. Chill in refrigerator several hours or overnight.

16 to 20 servings

Cheese Cake

1 cup sifted all-purpose flour
2 tablespoons sugar
¼ teaspoon salt
¼ cup softened butter
1 egg, slightly beaten
2¼ cups (about 12 oz.) blanched almonds (about 5⅓ cups, grated)
1 16-oz. can pitted tart red cherries
1 lb. (2 cups, firmly packed) dry cottage cheese
1 cup butter
2 teaspoons grated lemon peel
1 cup sugar
7 egg yolks, well beaten
7 egg whites
¾ cup sugar

1. Set out a 9-in. spring-form pan.
2. *For Crust*—Sift flour, sugar, and salt together into a bowl.
3. Make a well in center of dry ingredients; put butter and egg into well and work to a creamy mixture.
4. Work until dry ingredients are well blended. Shape dough into ball and wrap in waxed paper. Set in refrigerator to chill about 2 hrs. Put dough onto a lightly floured surface and flatten. Roll from center to edge into a round about ¼ in. thick. With knife or spatula, loosen pastry from surface whenever sticking occurs; lift pastry slightly and sprinkle flour under it.
5. With spatula, loosen pastry from surface and fold it in half, then in quarters. Gently lay it in pan and unfold pastry without stretching, fitting it to bottom of pan only.
6. Bake at 450°F 10 min.
7. Set aside on cooling rack to cool.
8. *For Filling*—Grate blanched almonds and set aside.
9. Set cherries aside to drain thoroughly.
10. Force cottage cheese through a sieve or food mill into a bowl and set aside.
11. Cream together butter and lemon peel until butter is softened.
12. Add 1 cup sugar gradually, creaming until fluffy after each addition.
13. Add egg yolks gradually, creaming until fluffy after each addition.
14. Beat in the cheese and almonds. Set aside.
15. Lightly butter the sides of the spring-form pan.
16. Beat egg whites until frothy.
17. Add ¾ cup sugar gradually, beating well after each addition.
18. Continue beating until very stiff peaks are formed. Spread beaten egg whites over cheese mixture and gently fold together. Arrange the well-drained cherries in an even layer over the cooled crust. Gently turn the cheese mixture into the pan; spread evenly.
19. Bake at 300°F about 1 hr. and 30 min. Turn off heat; let stand in oven 1 hr. longer.
20. Remove to cooling rack to cool completely (about 4 hrs.). Set in refrigerator to chill. Carefully run a spatula around inside of pan from top to bottom to loosen cake. Remove sides of pan. If desired, sprinkle edge of Cheese Cake with sifted **confectioners' sugar**.

About 16 servings

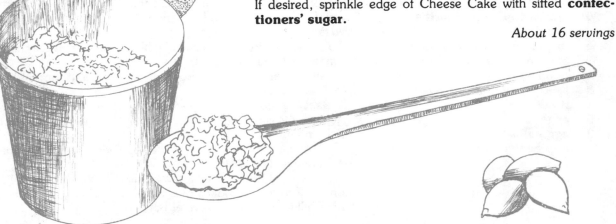

Cheese Pastry for 2-Crust Pie

2   **cups sifted all-purpose flour**

1   **teaspoon salt**

4   **oz. Cheddar cheese (about 1 cup, grated)**

⅔   **cup lard, hydrogenated vegetable shortening or all-purpose shortening**

5   **tablespoons cold water**

1. Set out an 8-or 9-inch pie pan.
2. Sift flour and salt together in a bowl.
3. Grate Cheddar cheese and mix into flour mixture.
4. Cut hydrogenated vegetable shortening or all-purpose shortening in with pastry blender or two knives until pieces are size of small peas.
5. Sprinkle water over mixture, a teaspoon at a time.
6. Mix lightly with a fork after each addition. Add only enough water to hold pastry together. Work quickly and do not overhandle. Divide dough into halves and shape each into a ball.
7. For bottom crust, flatten one ball of pastry on a lightly floured surface. Roll from center to edge into a round about 1/8 in., thick and about 1 in. larger than over-all size of pan. With knife or spatula, loosen pastry from surface whenever sticking occurs; lift pastry slightly and sprinkle flour underneath. Loosen one half of pastry and fold over other half; loosen remaining part and fold into quarters. Gently lift pastry into pan and unfold it, fitting it to the pan without stretching. Trim pastry around rim of pan with a sharp knife. Do not prick.
8. Roll second ball of pastry for upper crust. Slit it with knife in several places to permit escape of steam during baking. Fold in half.
9. Fill pie as desired.
10. Moisten edge of bottom crust with water for a tight seal. Carefully lay top crust over filling and unfold. Trim with scissors about ½ in. beyond edge of rim. Fold extra top pastry under edge of bottom pastry and flute or press edges together with a fork.
11. Bake as directed.

Pastry for one 8- or 9-in. 2-crust pie

Cheese Pastry for 1-Crust Pie: Follow recipe for Cheese Pastry for 2-Crust Pie. Reduce Cheddar cheese to 2 oz. (½ cup, grated), flour to 1 cup, salt to ½ teaspoon, shortening to ⅓ cup and water to about 2½ tablespoons. Roll out full amount of pastry for bottom crust, gently fit into pan without stretching and trim with scissors ½ inch beyond edge of rim. Fold extra pastry under at edge and flute or press with a fork. Thoroughly prick bottom and sides of pastry shell with a fork. (Omit pricking if filling is to be baked in shell.)

Bake at 450°F 10 to 15 min., or until crust is light golden brown. Cool on cooling rack before filling.

Cheese Pastry for 1-Crust 10-in. Pie: Follow recipe for **Cheese Pastry for 1-Crust Pie,** but use 3 oz. cheese (¾ cup, grated), 1⅓ cups flour, ¾ teaspoon salt, ½ cup shortening and about 3 tablespoons water. Fit into 10-in. pie pan.

Basic Pastry: Follow Recipe for Cheese Pastry for 2-Crust Pie or any variations, omitting the Cheddar cheese.

Dramatic Cheese Cake

½   **lb. chocolate wafers (or enough to yield 2¼ cups crumbs)**
¼   **cup sifted confectioners' sugar**
¼   **cup butter or margarine, softened**
1   **lb. (about 2 cups, firmly packed) dry cottage cheese**
½   **cup cold water**
1   **env. unflavored gelatin**
3   **egg yolks, slightly beaten**
⅔   **cup sugar**
¼   **cup cream**
2   **teaspoons grated lemon peel**
1½   **teaspoons vanilla extract**
½   **cup chilled whipping cream**
3   **egg whites**
½   **cup sugar**

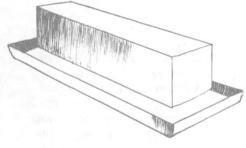

1. Set out a 7-in. spring-form pan. Put a hand rotary beater and a bowl in refrigerator to chill.
2. *For Crust*—Prepare crumbs from chocolate wafers.
3. Reserve 1¼ cups crumbs to coat cake. Turn remaining 1 cup crumbs into a medium-size bowl; add and stir in confectioners' sugar.
4. Using fork or pastry blender, blend in butter or margarine.
5. With fingers or back of spoon, press crumb mixture very firmly into an even layer on bottom of pan. Let stand at room temperature while preparing filling.
6. *For Filling*—Force cottage cheese through a food mill or a sieve into a bowl and set aside.
7. Pour water into a small cup or custard cup.
8. Sprinkle unflavored gelatin evenly over water.
9. Let gelatin stand until softened.
10. Meanwhile, blend well egg yolks, sugar and cream in top of double boiler.
11. Cook over simmering water, stirring constantly and rapidly, until mixture thickens. Remove from heat and strain into a bowl. Immediately blend in softened gelatin, stirring until gelatin is completely dissolved. Add the cottage cheese all at one time and blend thoroughly.
12. Mix in lemon peel and vanilla extract.
13. Using chilled bowl and beater, beat whipping cream until cream is of medium consistency (piles softly).
14. Blend into cottage cheese mixture; set aside.
15. Beat egg whites until frothy.
16. Add ½ cup sugar gradually, beating well after each addition.
17. Continue beating until very stiff peaks are formed. Spread egg whites over cheese mixture and gently fold together.
18. Spoon filling evenly over crust. Sift one half of remaining crumbs over top. Place in refrigerator for 10 to 12 hrs., or until firm.
19. Carefully run a spatula around inside of pan, from top to bottom, to loosen cake. Remove sides of pan. Do not remove cake from bottom of pan. Turn reserved crumbs into a long sheet of waxed paper. Set cake on paper next to crumbs. With wide spatula or spoon, toss crumbs onto sides of cake, coating completely. Return to refrigerator until serving time.
20. If desired, decorate by forcing **Sweetened Whipped Cream** through a pastry bag and No. 27 star tube.

12 to 14 servings

Pineapple Cheese Cake

24	graham crackers (or enough to yield 1¾ cups crumbs)
¼	cup sugar
½	cup butter or margarine, softened
1	15¼-oz. can crushed pineapple (about 1½ cups, drained)
12	oz. cream cheese, softened
½	teaspoon vanilla, extract
½	cup sugar (adding gradually)
⅛	teaspoon cinnamon
2	eggs, slightly beaten
1	cup thick sour cream
3	tablespoons sugar
1	teaspoon vanilla extract

1. Butter bottom and sides of one 9-in. round layer cake pan with removable bottom.
2. *For Crust*—Prepare crumbs from graham crackers.
3. Turn crumbs into a bowl. Stir in ¼ cup sugar.
4. Using a fork or pastry blender, blend in butter or margarine.
5. Using back of spoon, press crumb mixture very firmly into an even layer on bottom and sides of the pan. Bake at 375°F 5 min. Cool.
6. *For Filling*—Drain pineapple, reserving syrup for use in other food preparation.
7. Put into a bowl and blend cream cheese and vanilla extract together.
8. Add ½ cup sugar, cinnamon, and eggs in order, blending until smooth after each addition.
9. Gently blend in the crushed pineapple. Turn filling into the crumb crust in pan.
10. Bake at 325°F 35 min.
11. Meanwhile mix sour cream, 3 tablespoons sugar, and vanilla together.
12. Spread sour cream mixture on top of cake. Cool completely. Set in refrigerator to chill thoroughly before serving.

12 servings

Cottage Cheese Pie à l'Aristocrate

	Basic Pastry (page 61;use 10-in. pie pan)
3	cups cake crumbs
½	cup butter
1	teaspoon grated lemon peel
¾	teaspoon cinnamon
½	teaspoon nutmeg
¼	teaspoon salt
½	cup sugar
2	egg yolks, well beaten
1	cup firmly packed dry cottage cheese
3	tablespoons sherry
3	tablespoons brandy
1	cup cream (adding gradually)
4	egg whites

1. Prepare Basic Pastry, bake at 450°F for 10 min., and set aside to cool.
2. *For Filling*—Crumble enough cake to yield 3 cups cake crumbs.
3. Set crumbs aside.
4. Cream butter, lemon peel, cinnamon, nutmeg, and salt together until butter is softened.
5. Add sugar gradually, creaming until fluffy after each addition.
6. Add egg yolks gradually, beating well after each addition.
7. Add and beat cottage cheese until curds are slightly broken.
8. Stir cake crumbs into creamed mixture.
9. Add in order, sherry, brandy, and cream, mixing well after each addition.
10. Beat egg whites until stiff (not dry) peaks are formed.
11. Spread beaten egg whites over cottage-cheese mixture and fold together. Turn mixture into the pastry shell.
12. Bake at 350°F about 50 min., or until filling is set.
13. Serve pie slightly warm.

One 10-in. pie

Lemon-Cheese Pie

Crumb Crust (See Plum-Glazed Cheese Pie, page 66. Use 16 to 18 graham crackers and decrease sugar and butter or margarine to ¼ cup each; reserve 2 tablespoons crumb mixture for topping)

9 oz. cream cheese, softened
2 tablespoons butter or margarine
½ teaspoon vanilla extract
½ cup sugar
1 egg, slightly beaten
2 tablespoons all-purpose flour
⅔ cup milk
¼ cup lemon juice
2 tablespoons grated lemon peel

1. Set out an 8-in. pie pan.
2. *For Crust*—Prepare but do not bake Crumb Crust.
3. *For Filling*—Mix together cream cheese, butter or margarine, and vanilla extract until thoroughly blended.
4. Add in order, ½ cup sugar, egg, flour, milk, lemon juice, and lemon peel, blending until smooth after each addition.
5. Turn filling into prepared pie shell. Sprinkle reserved crumb mixture over top of pie to form a decorative pattern.
6. Bake at 325°F 35 min. Remove from oven and cool on cooling rack.
7. Chill in refrigerator until ready to serve.

One 8-in. pie

Note: For interesting flavor variation, omit crumb garnish on top and spread baked pie with thick **sour cream.**

American Glory Apple-Cheese Pie

Cheese Pastry for 2-Crust Pie (page 61; use 9-in. pie pan)

4 graham crackers (or enough to yield ⅓ cup crumbs)
4 oz. Cheddar cheese (about 1 cup, grated)
8 medium-size apples (about 6 cups sliced)
2 teaspoons lemon juice
¾ cup sugar
2 tablespoons all-purpose flour
½ teaspoon cinnamon
½ teaspoon nutmeg
⅛ teaspoon salt
2 tablespoons butter or margarine

1. Prepare and set aside Cheese Pastry.
2. Crush graham crackers and set aside.
3. Grate Cheddar cheese and set aside.
4. Wash apples, quarter, core, pare and thinly slice.
5. Sprinkle lemon juice evely over apples.
6. Toss a mixture of sugar, flour, cinnamon, nutmeg, and salt gently with apples.
7. Sprinkle graham cracker crumbs evenly over bottom of pastry shell. Spoon one third of apple mixture in an even layer into pastry shell. Top with one half of the grated cheese. Beginning with apples, repeat layers and end with apples. Slightly heap the last layer of apples in the center. Dot with butter or margarine.
8. Complete as in Pastry for 2-Crust Pie.
9. Bake at 450°F 10 min. Reduce heat to 350°F and bake about 40 min. longer, or until crust is light golden brown.
10. Serve warm or cold.

One 9-in. pie

Little Princess Fried Pies

Cheese Pastry for 2-Crust Pie (page 61, double recipe; no pie pan will be needed)

6 medium-size (about 2 lbs.) cooking apples (about 6 cups, diced)

⅓ cup hot water

4 oz. Cheddar cheese (about 1 cup, grated)

⅔ cup sugar

1½ teaspoons cinnamon

½ teaspoon nutmeg

2 tablespoons butter

4 teaspoons lemon juice

4 tablespoons lard, hydrogenated vegetable shortening or all-purpose shortening

1. Prepare, shape into 2 balls (do not roll) and set aside Cheese Pastry.
2. Set out a 2-qt. saucepan having a tight-fitting cover, and a heavy 10-in. skillet.
3. Wash apples, quarter, core, pare and coarsely dice.
4. Put apples in the saucepan with hot water.
5. Cover and simmer, moving and turning apple pieces occasionally, 5 to 10 min., or until apples are just tender when pierced with a fork. Drain thoroughly.
6. While the apples are cooking, grate Cheddar cheese.
7. Mix ½ to ⅔ cup sugar, 1½ teaspoons cinnamon, and ½ teaspoon nutmeg with cheese and set aside.
8. Add to the drained, cooked apples, butter and lemon juice.
9. Add the cheese mixture and stir only enough to mix ingredients evenly. Set aside.
10. Flatten one ball of pastry on a lightly floured surface. Roll from center to edge into a round about 1/8 in. thick. With knife or spatula, loosen pastry from surface whenever sticking occurs; lift pastry slightly and sprinkle flour underneath.
11. Cut out 6-in. rounds, using a saucer or a waxed paper pattern as a guide. Spoon about 2 tablespoons of the apple filling onto one half of each round. Moisten the edge of one half of the round with water to help form a tight seal and fold other half of round over the filling. Press edges together with a fork. Be certain that the seal is tight and pastry unbroken to avoid leaking of filling.
12. Repeat with the remaining ball of pastry.
13. Heat lard, hydrogenated vegetable shortening or all-purpose shortening in the skillet over medium heat.
14. Carefully put into the skillet as many pies as will fit in without crowding. Fry pies on one side about 5 min., or until golden brown. Turn and fry until other side is golden brown. Add more shortening to skillet if necessary to keep pies from sticking.
15. Serve warm with slices of **sharp cheese,** a dip of **ice cream** or a mound of **whipped cream;** or sift **confectioners' sugar** over the pies.

12 to 14 pies

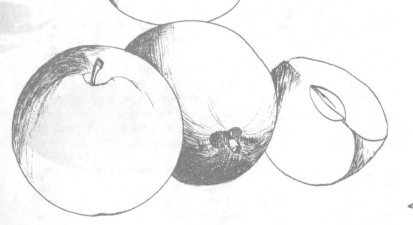

Plum-Glazed Cheese Pie

22	graham crackers (or enough to yield 1⅔ cups crumbs)
5	tablespoons sugar
⅛	teaspoon salt
5	tablespoons butter or margarine, softened
8	oz. cream cheese, softened
½	cup sweetened condensed milk
2	tablespoons lemon juice
1	teaspoon grated lemon peel
¼	teaspoon vanilla extract
½	cup chilled whipping cream
1	lb. fresh Italian plums
1	cup sugar
¾	cup water
1½	teaspoons cornstarch

1. Set out a 10-in. pie pan. Set a bowl and rotary beater in refrigerator to chill.
2. *For Crust*—Prepare crumbs from graham crackers.
3. Turn crumbs into a medium size bowl. Stir in sugar and salt.
4. Using a fork or pastry blender, blend in butter or margarine.
5. Using back of spoon, press crumb mixture very firmly into an even layer on bottom and sides of the pie pan. Level edges of pie shell.
6. Bake at 375°F 8 min. Set on cooling rack to cool completely.
7. *For Filling*—Put cream cheese into a bowl.
8. Add condensed milk, lemon juice, lemon peel and vanilla extract gradually and blend in thoroughly.
9. Using the chilled bowl and beater, beat whipping cream until cream is of medium consistency (piles softly).
10. Fold the whipped cream into the cream-cheese mixture. Turn into the pie shell and set in refrigerator to chill.
11. *For Glaze*—Wash Italian plums thoroughly and drain.
12. Cut into halves; remove and discard pits. Set plums aside.
13. Combine 1 cup sugar and water in a saucepan.
14. Set over medium heat; stir until sugar is dissolved. Bring to boiling. Cover and boil gently 5 min. Add the plum halves to the syrup and cook slowly until just tender. Remove from heat; cool plum halves in syrup. Using a slotted spoon, carefully remove plums to a shallow dish or pan. Reserve the syrup.
15. Put cornstarch into a small saucepan.
16. Add gradually, blending in, ½ cup of the reserved syrup. Stirring gently and constantly, bring rapidly to boiling and cook for 3 min., or until mixture is transparent. Set aside to cool.
17. Arrange the cooled plum halves, cut sides down, on top of the filling. Spoon the glaze (cooled syrup mixture) over plums, and filling. Set in refrigerator to chill thoroughly before serving.

One 10-in. pie

Orange-Banana Cheese Pie: Follow recipe for Plum-Glazed Cheese Pie for Crumb Crust and Filling. Using a sharp knife, cut away peel from 1 **orange.** Remove sections by cutting on each side of dividing membrane, working over a bowl to save juice. Remove and discard seeds, if any. Peel 2 **bananas** with brown-flecked peel. Score by pulling tines of a fork down the bananas lengthwise. Repeat until entire surface is scored. Cut the scored bananas, on a slant, into ¼-in. slices. Brush with **lemon juice** to prevent darkening. To prepare a glaze, mix in a saucepan 6 tablespoons **sugar** and 2 teaspoons **cornstarch.** Stir in 3 tablespoons **orange juice,** 2 tablespoons **water** and 2 teaspoons **lemon juice.** Stirring gently and constantly, bring mixture rapidly to boiling and cook for 3 min., or until mixture is transparent. Set aside to cool.

On top of the chilled filling, arrange 3 of the banana slices, slightly overlapping, from edge toward center of pie. Place an orange section next to slices, parallel to them. Repeat process, alternating the orange sections and banana slices around the pie to form a fruit ring. Spoon the cooled glaze over the fruit and filling. Set in refrigerator to chill thoroughly before serving. Garnish with **mint sprigs.**

Strawberry-Glazed Cheese Pie: Follow recipe for Plum-Glazed Cheese Pie for crust and filling. Set out 16-oz. pkg. frozen **strawberries** to thaw. Drain strawberries thoroughly, reserving syrup. Put 2 teaspoons **cornstarch** into a small saucepan. Gradually add ¾ cup of the reserved strawberry syrup, stirring until smooth. Stirring gently and constantly, bring rapidly to boiling and cook for 3 min., or until mixture is transparent. Set aside to cool for about 10 min. Gently blend in the strawberries. Spoon glaze over pie and set in refrigerator to chill.

Cannoli (Cream Rolls)

3	cups (about 1½ lbs.) Ricotta cheese
1⅓	cups sugar
2	teaspoons vanilla extract
½	cup (about 3 oz.) finely chopped candied citron
⅓	cup semi-sweet chocolate pieces
3	cups sifted all-purpose flour
¼	cup sugar
1	teaspoon cinnamon
¼	teaspoon salt
3	tablespoons shortening
2	eggs, well beaten
2	tablespoons white vinegar
2	tablespoons cold water
½	cup pistachio nuts Egg white, slightly beaten

1. Set out 6 6-in. aluminum tubes)about ¾ in. in diameter). A deep saucepan or an automatic deep fryer will be needed.
2. *For Filling*—Combine Ricotta cheese, 1⅓ cups sugar and vanilla extract and beat until smooth (about 10 min. with an electric mixer on medium-high speed.
3. Add citron and chocolate pieces and mix thoroughly.
4. Put mixture in refrigerator to chill.
5. *For Shells*—Sift flour, sugar, cinnamon, and salt together into a bowl.
6. Cut shortening in with pastry blender or two knives until mixture resembles cornmeal.
7. Stir in eggs.
8. Blend in white vinegar and water, one tablespoon at a time.
9. Turn dough onto a lightly floured surface and knead. Wrap in waxed paper and chill in refrigerator for at least 30 min.
10. About 20 min. before deep frying fill the saucepan or deep fry with fat and heat to 365°F.
11. Cut a 6x4½-in. oval pattern from waxed paper.
12. Blanch pistachio nuts, finely chop and set aside.
13. Using a small amount at a time, roll chilled dough 1/16 to 1/8 in. thick on floured surface. With waxed paper pattern and a pastry cutter, cut ovals from dough.
14. Wrap ovals loosely around the aluminum tubes, lapping over opposite edges. Brush edges with egg white.
15. Press edges together to seal.
16. Deep fry shells in heated fat. Fry only as many shells at one time as will lie uncrowded one layer deep in the fat. Fry about 8 min., or until golden brown. Turn occasionally with a fork during frying (do not pierce). Using tongs or slotted spoon, drain shells over fat a few seconds; remove to absorbent paper. Cool slightly; remove tubes. Cool completely.
17. When ready to serve, fill with the Ricotta filling. Sprinkle ends of Cannoli with the chopped nuts and sprinkle shells with sifted confectioners' sugar.

About 16 to 18 Cannoli

Marbled Brownies

1½ **tablespoons butter or margarine**
½ **teaspoon vanilla extract**
3 **tablespoons sugar**
2 **teaspoons cornstarch**
⅔ **cup dry cottage cheese**
1 **egg, well beaten**
1 **tablespoon milk**
⅛ **teaspoon salt**
2 **sq. (2 oz.) chocolate**
1 **cup sifted cake flour**
½ **teaspoon baking powder**
½ **teaspoon salt**
1 **cup (about 4 oz.) nuts**
½ **cup shortening**
½ **teaspoon vanilla extract**
1 **cup sugar**
2 **eggs, well beaten**

1. Grease a 9x9x2-in. pan.
2. *For Cheese Mixture*—Cream together butter or margarine and vanilla extract until butter is softened.
3. Add 3 tablespoons sugar gradually, creaming until fluffy after each addition.
4. Blend in cornstarch, cottage cheese, egg, milk, and salt, in order.
5. Set aside.
6. *For Brownies*—Melt chocolate and set aside.
7. Sift together flour, baking powder, and salt.
8. Chop nuts and set aside.
9. Cream shortening and vanilla extract together until shortening is softened.
10. Add 1 cup sugar gradually, creaming until fluffy after each addition.
11. Add eggs in thirds, beating thoroughly after each addition.
12. Stir in chocolate. Mixing well after each addition, blend in dry ingredients in fourths. Stir in the nuts. Spread one half of dough in pan. Spread Cheese Mixture over chocolate layer. Spread remaining dough over cheese. Draw spoon through layers until marbled effect is produced.
13. Bake at 375°F 40 to 45 min., or until wooden pick or cake tester inserted in center comes out clean.
14. Cool in pan and cut into squares.

16 brownies

Date-Filled Cookies

4 **oz. sharp Cheddar cheese (about 1 cup, grated)**
1¼ **cups sifted all-purpose flour**
⅛ **teaspoon salt**
½ **cup butter or margarine**
½ **teaspoon vanilla extract**
½ **cup (about 3 oz.) finely cut dates**
¼ **cup (about 1 oz.) finely chopped pecans**
3 **tablespoons brown sugar**
3 **tablespoons water**

1. Set out cookie sheets.
2. Grate Cheddar cheese and set aside.
3. Sift together flour and salt and set aside.
4. Cream together butter or margarine and vanilla extract until softened.
5. Blend in the grated cheese. Mixing well after each addition, add dry ingredients in fourths. Wrap dough in waxed paper and chill until easy to handle.
6. Meanwhile, prepare dates and pecans.
7. Put dates into a saucepan with brown sugar and water.
8. Cook over low heat, stirring constantly, until thick and blended, about 5 min. Stir in nuts. Set filling aside to cool.
9. Put chilled dough on a lightly floured surface. Roll dough into a 16x12-in. rectangle about 1/8-in. thick. Cut dough into halves. Spread one half of dough with cooled filling and top with remaining dough. Cut into 2-in. squares. Transfer to cookie sheets. Press all edges of cookies with a fork to seal.
10. Bake at 350°F about 12 to 15 min., or until edges are light brown.

About 2 doz. cookies

Cream Cheese Crepes

1	tablespoon butter
1	cup sifted all-purpose flour
2	tablespoons sugar
¼	teaspoon salt
6	oz. cream cheese
3	eggs, well beaten
1½	cups milk
1	teaspoon grated orange peel
	Confectioners' sugar

1. Melt butter in a 6-in. skillet and set aside to cool.
2. Sift flour, sugar and salt together into a bowl and set aside.
3. Beat cream cheese until fluffy.
4. Blend in eggs until smooth.
5. Beat in the melted butter and orange peel.
6. Combine egg mixture with dry ingredients and beat with rotary beater until smooth.
7. Heat skillet; it is hot enough when a few drops cold water dropped on it dance rapidly in small beads. Pour in about 2 tablespoons batter for each crepe. Immediately tilt skillet back and forth to spread batter thinly and evenly. Cook each crepe over medium heat until lightly browned on bottom and firm to touch on top. Loosen edges with spatula. Turn and brown second side. (It should be unnecessary to grease the skillet for each crepe.)
8. As each crepe is cooked transfer it to a hot platter. Roll up the crepes and set them in oven to keep warm. When all are cooked, sift confectioners' sugar over tops.

6 to 8 servings

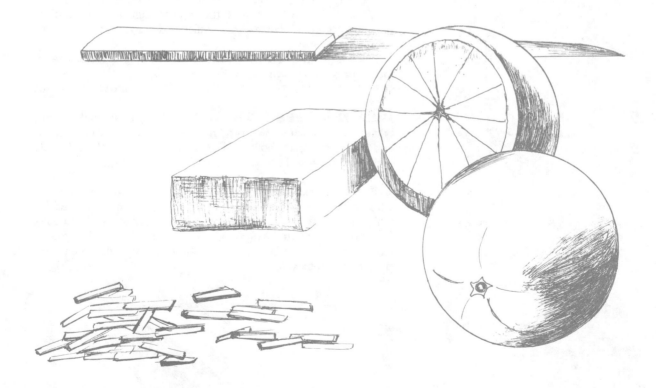

Cheese Blintzes

1½ **cups cream-style cottage cheese, drained**
¼ **cup thick sour cream**
1½ **tablespoons sugar**
½ **teaspoon salt**
2 **tablespoons butter or margarine**
1½ **cups sifted all-purpose flour**
3 **tablespoons sugar**
½ **teaspoon salt**
2 **eggs**
1¼ **cups milk**
Butter or margarine
1 **tablespoon butter or margarine**

1. Set out heavy 6- and 10-in. skillets.
2. *For Filling*—Mix cottage cheese, sour cream, 1½ tablespoons sugar, and ½ teaspoon salt thoroughly and set aside in refrigerator.
3. *For Pancakes*—Melt butter or margarine and set aside to cool.
4. Sift flour, 3 tablespoons sugar, and ½ teaspoon salt together into a bowl and set aside.
5. Beat eggs until thick and piled softly.
6. Beat milk in the melted butter.
7. Combine egg mixture with dry ingredients. With rotary beater, beat until smooth and well blended. Set aside.
8. Heat the small skillet; it is hot enough when a few drops of water sprinkled on surface dance in small beads. Grease skillet lightly with butter or margarine.
9. Pour only enough batter to coat skillet thinly; immediately tilt skillet back and forth to spread batter evenly. Cook pancake over medium heat about 2 min., or until lightly browned on bottom and firm to touch on top. With spatula, remove pancake to a plate, brown side up. Stack pancakes. (It should not be necessary to grease skillet for each pancake.)
10. *For Blintzes*—Spoon about 1½ tablespoons filling into center of brown side of one pancake. Fold two opposite sides of pancake to center. Begin with one of the open sides and roll. Press edge to seal. Repeat process for each pancake.
11. Heat butter or margarine in the large skillet.
12. Arrange several blintzes in skillet, sealed sides down. Brown on all sides over medium heat, turning carefully with two spoons or tongs. Remove blintzes from skillet and place on serving platter.
13. Serve hot with **currant jelly** or **blueberry** or **blackberry jam** and **sour cream.**

About 12 blintzes

Raisin-Cheese Blintzes: Bring to boiling ½ cup **water;** add to water ¼ cup **dark seedless** or **golden raisins** and again bring to boiling. Drain raisins thoroughly. Follow recipe for Cheese Blintzes. Mix raisins with Filling.

Caramel-Cheese Blintzes: Follow recipe for Cheese Blintzes. After blintzes are removed from skillet, add 3 tablespoons **butter** or **margarine** to same skillet. Add 1¼ cups firmly packed **brown sugar.** Cook over low heat, stirring until sugar is dissolved. Mix in ¼ cup **Cointreau.** When sauce is hot, pour over blintzes.

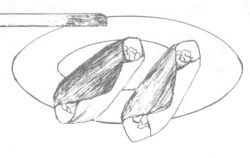

Lemon-Cheese Ice Cream

6	oz. cream cheese
⅔	cup sugar
2	cups chilled cream
2	tablespoons lemon juice
1	teaspoon grated lemon peel
¼	teaspoon vanilla extract

1. Set refrigerator control at coldest operating temperature. Put a bowl, rotary beater and refrigerator tray into refrigerator to chill.
2. Beat cream cheese until fluffy.
3. Add sugar gradually, creaming after each addition.
4. Add cream, lemon juice, lemon peel, and vanilla extract gradually, mixing thoroughly.
5. Turn into refrigerator tray and place in freezing compartment of refrigerator. Freeze until mushy.
6. Turn mixture into the chilled bowl and beat with chilled beater until smooth. Return to refrigerator tray and freeze until firm.

About 1 qt. ice cream

Vanilla-Almond Ice Cream: Follow recipe for Lemon-Cheese Ice Cream. Omit lemon juice and grated peel. Increase vanilla extract to 1 tablespoon. Mix in ½ cup (3 oz.) coarsely chopped toasted **almonds** before turning into refrigerator tray.

Maraschino Cherry Special: Follow recipe for Lemon-Cheese Ice Cream. Omit lemon peel. Decrease lemon juice to 2 teaspoons and increase vanilla extract to 1 teaspoon. Mix in ½ cup coarsely chopped **maraschino cherries,** well drained, before turning into refrigerator tray.

Edam Cheese Topping

1	Edam cheese (about 1 lb.)
¼	cup (about 1 oz.) pecans
1	cup cream
	Pecan halves

1. Set out Edam cheese to soften at room temperature.
2. Meanwhile, coarsely chop pecans and set aside.
3. When cheese is softened, cut a thin slice from the top, through the wax coating. Hollow out the cheese, leaving a ¼-in. shell. Set cheese shell aside.
4. Crumble the cheese into a bowl. Cover with cream.
5. Beat until fluffy. Blend in the chopped pecans. Spoon the mixture into the cheese shell. Garnish with pecan halves.
6. Serve as an accompaniment to apple, mince or pumpkin pie.

About 2½ cups topping

Note: If you prefer a larger Edam cheese for your centerpiece, soften only part of the cheese with cream and refill shell. If there is any sauce remaining after serving, scrape it away, rewrap cheese and store.

Cream Cheese Topping

6   oz. cream cheese
1   cup sifted confectioners'
    sugar
5   tablespoons milk or cream
½   teaspoon almond extract

1. Beat cream cheese until very fluffy.
2. Add confectioners' sugar gradually to cream cheese, beating until fluffy after each addition.
3. Add and beat milk or cream and almond extract until smooth.
4. Cover mixture and put in the refrigerator to chill thoroughly.
5. Serve in a chilled serving bowl as a topping for warm apple pie.

About 1⅓ cups topping

Rich Cheese Sauce for Apple Pie

6   oz. sharp process Cheddar
    cheese food
½   cup milk

1. Put Cheddar cheese in top of double boiler.
2. Place over simmering water and stir constantly until cheese begins to melt. Add milk gradually while stirring constantly.
3. Continue to stir constantly until cheese is melted and mixture is smooth.
4. Serve piping hot over apple pie.

About 1 cup sauce

Cheese-Pineapple Dessert Platter

1   whole pineapple
2   5-oz. jars process cheese
    spread with pineapple
3   tablespoons milk
2   tablespoons finely chopped
    maraschino cherries,
    drained
1   "Baby" Gouda cheese
    Swiss cheese slices

1. Wash and cut pineapple into halves lengthwise through the crown (spiny top).
2. Using a sharp knife, cut out and discard core sections. Remove pineapple from shells with a grapefruit knife or sharp paring knife. Cut pineapple into bite-sized chunks and set aside.
3. Blend together contents of process cheese spread, milk, and maraschino cherries.
4. Pile one half of the cheese filling into each pineapple shell.
5. Cut into wedges "Baby" Gouda cheese.
6. *To Arrange Platter*—Place filled pineapple shells, end to end, in center of platter. Spear pineapple chunks with wooden or cocktail picks, and arrange around sides of cheese filling. Following edge of platter, arrange Swiss cheese slices overlapping, to form a border.
7. Arrange Gouda cheese wedges in overlapping rows around pineapple shells. Serve with crisp **crackers.**

Lemon Cream Cheese Frosting

6 oz. cream cheese, softened
1½ teaspoons lemon juice
½ teaspoon grated lemon peel
4 cups sifted confectioners' sugar
Milk or cream

1. Blend cream cheese, lemon juice, and lemon peel together.
2. Add confectioners' sugar gradually and blend in.
3. If frosting is too stiff to spread, blend in milk or cream, 1 teaspoon at a time, until easy to spread.

Enough to frost sides and tops of two 9-in. round cake layers.

Orange Cream Cheese Frosting: Follow recipe for Lemon Cream Cheese Frosting. Omit lemon juice and lemon peel. Blend with the cream cheese 2 tablespoons plus 2 teaspoons thawed frozen **orange juice concentrate.** Chill frosting in refrigerator until of spreading consistency (about 30 min.). Store frosted cake in refrigerator.

Chocolate Cream Cheese Frosting: Follow recipe for Lemon Cream Cheese Frosting. Omit lemon juice and lemon peel. Blend with the cream cheese 1 teaspoon **vanilla extract.** After sugar has been added, blend in 2 oz. (2 sq.) **chocolate** which has been melted and cooled.

Quick Chocolate Fudge

4 oz. (4 sq.) chocolate
¾ cup (about 3 oz.) nuts
6 oz. cream cheese, softened
4¼ cups sifted confectioners' sugar
1 tablespoon vanilla extract

1. Butter and 8x8x2-in. pan.
2. Melt chocolate and set aside to cool.
3. Coarsely chop nuts and set aside.
4. Beat cream cheese until fluffy.
5. Add confectioners' sugar gradually, beating until fluffy after each addition.
6. Blend in thoroughly the cooled chocolate and vanilla extract.
7. Stir in the nuts. Turn into the buttered pan. Chill in refrigerator until firm.
8. Cut into 1½-in. squares.

About 2 doz. pieces fudge

Coconut Fudge: Follow recipe for Quick Chocolate Fudge. Substitute ¾ cup moist, shredded **coconut,** cut, for the nuts.

Butter Pecan Fudge: Follow recipe for Quick Chocolate Fudge. Omit chocolate. Use **pecans** for the nuts, increase amount to 1 cup and toast before chopping.

Cheese and Fruit for Dessert

A dessert of cheese, fruit and crackers has everything—beauty, subtlety of flavor, gourmet elegance and scope for personal choice. It is the easiest of desserts to prepare and serve, yet few more elaborate ones can equal its appeal and its universal suitability.

Choose your handsomest tray to display the cheeses. Select both familiar and unusual cheeses with a variety of flavors and textures. Let them stand at room temperature for an hour or two before serving, to regain their full flavor and their natural texture (refrigeration hardens all cheese somewhat).

Classic choices for this type of service are soft **cream cheese,** usually served in the piece; gay red **Edams** or **Goudas** served whole with the top cut off, to be scooped out as desired, making a striking centerpiece for the tray; slim wedges of tangy **Roquefort,** luscious big triangles of pungent **Camembert,** thick slices of delicate **Swiss,** cubes or paper-thin slices of mild dark **goats'-milk cheese,** mild or sharp **Cheddar** in slices, fingers or triangles.

Arrange pieces of fruit on the same tray with the cheese; or heap whole fruit in a separate crystal bowl or on another tray or plate to accompany the cheese tray. Polished red and green **apples,** juicy **pears** rich red or purple or green **grapes,** all glowing like jewels, are particularly pleasing in their season. A charming and unusual type of fruit service to match the dramatic appeal of the cheese tray is fruit kabobs: ready-to-eat fruits—hulled fresh **strawberries,** fresh or canned **pineapple chunks,** seedless green **grapes, cantaloupe** and **honeydew melon** balls, sweet dark **cherries**—threaded on little metal skewers and arranged attractively on a nest of cracked ice in your loveliest crystal bowl. Smaller bowls of sparkling **fruit preserves** or especially interesting **jelly,** such as bar-le-duc, are appealing accompaniments for cheese and crackers when fresh fruits are not available; **candied fruits** and **peels** and **dried fruits** may also be used.

Be sure to serve plenty of crisp **crackers**—both salted and unsalted crackers, without competing flavors, to suit all tastes.

So that your guests may conveniently serve themselves, have a stack of your prettiest dessert plates at hand. Provide cheese cutters and scoops for any cheese that you put out in the whole piece; butter spreaders will be needed by all who choose **Camembert** or **cream cheese,** and sharp fruit knives by those who wish to cut their own fruit.

Blueberry Orange Cheese Cake

1½ cups graham cracker crumbs
2 tablespoons sugar
½ teaspoon cinnamon
½ teaspoon nutmeg
6 tablespoons butter, melted
4 cups cream-style cottage cheese
Heavy cream
6 eggs
1½ cups sugar
½ cup all-purpose flour
3 tablespoons thawed frozen orange juice concentrate
1 teaspoon vanilla extract
⅛ teaspoon salt
1 cup dairy sour cream
2 tablespoons confectioners' sugar
1 cup dry-pack frozen blueberries, thawed

1. Set out a 9-in. springform pan.
2. To prepare crust, combine graham cracker crumbs, sugar, cinnamon and nutmeg in a bowl.
3. Stir in butter.
4. Press the mixture on bottom and about three-fourths up sides of the springform pan. Chill crust while preparing the filling.
5. Drain cottage cheese (reserving the cream), press through a coarse sieve and set aside.
6. Measure reserved cream in a measuring cup for liquids and fill to 1-cup level with heavy cream.
7. In a large mixing bowl, beat eggs until very thick.
8. Add sugar, beating until light and fluffy.
9. Blend in the sieved cottage cheese, the cream and flour, orange juice concentrate, vanilla extract, and salt. Mix well and turn filling into crumb-lined pan.
10. Bake at 350°F oven 1 hr. and 10 to 20 min. (Cheese cake is done when a metal knife inserted near center comes out clean.)
11. While cake is baking, prepare topping. Combine sour cream, confectioners' sugar and blueberries in a small bowl.
12. When cake tests done, turn off heat. Open oven door and gently spread cake with topping mixture. Cool in oven until cake is of room temperature. Chill.

One 9-in. cheese cake

Note: Syrup-pack canned or frozen blueberries, drained, may be used in topping.

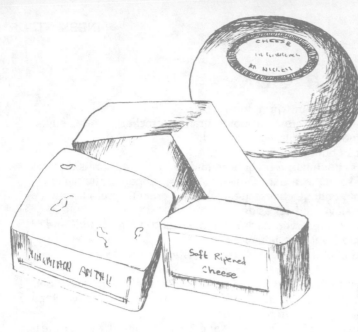
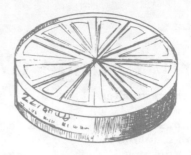

Cheese Index

Index